YEAR OF GRACE

YEAR OF GRACE
A Spiritual Journal

Andrew Greeley

THE THOMAS MORE PRESS
Chicago, Illinois

ISBN 0-88347-262-7

April 14, 1989

GRACIOUS LORD,

In reading Larry Cunningham's new book on prayer today and pondering his notion that prayer is the putting into words of our experience of God, it occurred to me that I write fine prayers for the characters in my stories and books, but I have trouble when I try to pray myself, because the distractions of fantastically and perhaps neurotically variegated life overwhelm.

Why do I not therefore make a virtue out of necessity and write out my prayers to You — who gives the experiences which make us want to pray and the power of prayer in response to that experience?

Writing my prayers, in effect keeping a religious journal (something about which I always thought but which I never seriously attempted before), would seem to be an excellent way of excluding distractions.

I have been working on a translation of the Hymn for Pentecost, the name of my most recent fictional effort, and finally made a breakthrough in it. I'll put the prayer here as my entry for the first day and as a prayer to the Holy Spirit as I begin this journal to help me pray in it.

Andrew Greeley

First, Blackie's Pentecost sermon which sets the context for the translation: "The Holy Spirit," Blackie Ryan peered out over his vast red chasuble at the Cathedral congregation, "is like Tinker Bell."

"You will remember Tinker Bell," the Monsignor continued, "a playful, dancing spirit in the Walt Disney version of Peter Pan, who flits blithely about, sparking into life with her magic wand all matter of wonders and surprises and enchantments. So too with the Spirit of God. She spins about creation, calling forth and presiding over variety and diversity and uniqueness. She is especially responsible for that which makes each creature most particularly itself, for the You that differentiates us one from another. If You disapprove of variety and thus disapprove of who You are, don't blame the Cathedral staff, don't even blame our good Cardinal. Blame God's spirit. On the other hand, if You enjoy the powerful attraction of those who are on the one hand unlike You and on the other hand like You, then on this special feast of the Spirit, offer Her gratitude for the splendid, attractive, overwhelming diversity of God's creation.

"If one has the choice of accepting and rejoicing in the variety with which God's Spirit has filled the world and resisting Her variety, one would be wise to accept and enjoy her playfulness. It is a mistake to try to fight the Holy Spirit."

Holy Spirit, come to us
Envelop us in heaven's trust
Wrap us in Your dazzling light
Come, O Father of the Poor

YEAR OF GRACE

Come, Giver of gifts most pure
Set our troubled hearts aright
Friend and trusted Advocate
Welcome Guest for whom we wait
Our refreshment cool and sweet
After work our precious rest
Goal of every frantic quest
In sorrow, the hope we need
O Light of surprise divine
Remember how short our time
Our strength and will please renew
Without Your help we are lost
Ignoble fluff not worth the cost
Our only hope lies in You
Heal whatever may be ill
Quicken that which may be still
Sooth my restless, aching heart
Revive that which may be old
Warm whatever may be cold
Bind us who have come apart
Protect us in love with You
Pardon all the wrong we may do
Grant us joy that does cease
Give us life's last reward
Bring us home to You, O Lord,
Grant us everlasting peace
Amen!

Alleluia!

Andrew Greeley

April 15

THE PSALM verse today says that the Lord put a new song in my heart and Saint Luke's Gospel tells the story of the shrewdness of the unjust steward. Appropriate for today, with a new song shaping in my head (I couldn't quite remember all the Latin of the Veni, so I called Dan Anzia, the only one I know in the world who would have a Latin graduale on the bookshelf) and he read it to me over the phone. We recited the last part of it together. The rhythms of the hymn echo and re-echo in my head, an old song made new. In the translation I'm trying to produce the same rhythms, no easy task.

Moreover with this journal I'm trying to be as shrewd as the steward, putting my strong suit, words on a blue and white screen, to use in prayer to You. Since the whole principle of the thing is that ideas come from You, directly or indirectly, You've put both the translation in my head and this technique for banishing distractions. How clever of You and thank You.

I should like all my work to be both a new and an old song. I'm not sure that my motivations have always been as pure as they might be (whose are?) but I got into this business with the intent to serve You and I hope that it is still the directive motive, however flawed by other motives it may be.

Help me to continue to be shrewd about praying and continue to be happy with a new song on my lips.

April 19

ONE of the shrewd things I've learned in the past couple of days is that I cannot put off these reflections until the last hour of my day. If I do, I'm too tired to write them out. They should rather be done first thing in the morning. Sunday I was in Chicago. Monday and Tuesday the computer was inoperative. Today I procrastinated and was busy about other things, including a breakdown of the machine. I also managed to take a chunk out of my finger with a knife on Monday while opening an English muffin, mostly as a result of weariness from the plane trip.

Anyway, I'm going to bed now. Tomorrow, right after my swim, I'll be at this machine, with Your help, trying to get my daily reflections back on track. Thank You for the help. I'm sorry I didn't do this earlier today.

April 20

7:47 AM

"Why art thou dejected, O my soul and disturbed within me?" Psalm 41.

"God be merciful to me a sinner" Luke 18.

"It would be nice to know;/but who can relive
their lives . . . ./The lost girls in a ring/on a
shadowy school playground/like the nymphs dancing together/ in the Allegory of Spring." Derek
Mahon.

Andrew Greeley

Derek Mahon imagines his first love, adored from a distance (as are all first loves), wonders what happened to her and her friends and laments that it is not possible to live one's life again—more likely that it is not possible to recapture the wonder and mystery of youth. It is an image to haunt anyone and to deject the soul. I review my own images from a similar time, realizing of course how time and a nostalgic patina make them more wonderful than they were when they were first recorded. They, nonetheless, represent the hope, the bright promise, the wonder, and the excitement of youth. When I consider what's happened since then I am disturbed and am prepared to cry out with the publican, "be merciful to me a sinner."

Mortality demands both dejection and a cry for mercy. No matter how much one has done with life, one has permitted so many opportunities to slip away. I realize now that I've spent the best winter (in terms of weather) in my decade here in Arizona without enjoying either the warm weather or a single sunset. Rather, most of my time has been spent in front of this machine or on airplanes. Sunset is a time when I must close the blinds so there isn't too much light to work on the computer. To miss one sunset that need not have been missed is to have lost an opportunity that will never recur. Such a moment cannot be prolonged but it can be remembered and thus be made eternal. In such moments You reveal Yourself, as in the hem of a garment sweeping across the sky and I realize that there is no reason for dejection and that the cry for mercy is in fact a cry for an opportunity to try again not to miss that which ought not to be missed.

Help me, gracious Lady, to revel in Your sunsets and, as best I can, in all the other traces of Your glory of which those bright moments of youth were only a faint hint. It is always, if one believes in You, the beginning of spring.

Against a desert sunset, however, it ceases to be a ground for dejection.

April 21

"LET the children come to me, for theirs is the kingdom of heaven."

"Thou hast saved us from our enemies" Psalm 43.

"Tacitus believed mariners could hear/the sun sinking into the western sea/and who would question that titanic roar/the steam rising wherever the edge may be" D. Mahon.

Mahon's poem is about imaginary worlds: the world is not only what we might observe but also what we might imagine. From a storyteller's point of view the imaginary world is as real as the other world even if it exists only in his head. The neat thing about that metaphor is that it suggests that God's imaginary worlds all become real. There are as many universes as God has imagined. If my friend George Coyne and the other astronomers are to be believed there are billions of such worlds.

I can accept that easily enough. As I said in my sonnet on Saint Patrick's Day, You are an exuberant youthful God and that's fine with me. But youth, exuberant youth, forgets, not because of malice but because there are so many things happening. How can a youthful God presiding exuberantly over a multi-cosmic universe find time to protect us from our enemies and thus require the trust that little children feel for their parents (which trust is what Jesus had in mind, I think, when he said that theirs is the kingdom of heaven)?

It was easier for David or whoever wrote the Psalms. They could imagine You intervening directly to smite the Philistines and the other unfriendlies who attacked them. In our day we believe that You are involved in providentially protecting Your friends through secondary causes. This means, I guess, that You and Your friends win in the long run but often that long run is the one Lord Keynes had in mind when he said that in the long run we are all dead.

In the short run, Your friends' enemies may well win and kill Your friends, just as Hitler, whose 100th birthday was yesterday, killed off six million of Your people and twenty or thirty million other people. I don't think that the problem of Your providence is any more serious after Auschwitz than it was before. It is serious enough, as Dylan Thomas said, that one innocent child be killed. After the death of a single innocent the triumph of evil is merely quantitative.

I'm forced to conclude that anyone who could imagine a multi-cosmic creation and bring that creation into being is capable of taking care of it all, youthful or not. It is less a leap of faith to accept Your existence than it is a leap of faith to accept Your power and love.

To return to the storyteller metaphor, just as I love the characters in my stories and, like William Kennedy, want salvation of one kind or another for all of them, so do

You love me and all the other characters You have imagined and thus brought into being. I must rely on You the way my creatures rely on me, I must trust You as little children trust their parents, even if they don't know quite how the parents will protect them.

Into thy hands I commend my spirit.

April 22

THE GOSPEL today is about the problems for the rich in entering the kingdom of heaven. In the Psalm David pleads again that You rescue us for Your mercy's sake. And Derek Mahon writes about a lighthouse, "It works both ways/of course, light/being, like love and the scold something that You/can give and keep/at the same time."

A nice contrast: the rather grim warning about the difficulty of avoiding worldly concerns (and the poorest of us would be counted rich by the standards of those who listened to Jesus), the psalmist, flat on his back pleading for help. And the playful Irish poet celebrating a lighthouse in Maine and seeing in it a hint of the mystery of love: You can give it and keep it at the same time.

I read yesterday Jack Haught's new book on revelation. Like everything he does, it's first rate. He sees human life as part of the unfolding drama of God's self-disclosure through creation, history, society, and personal life. Mystery remains because we cannot see the end of the process, just as earlier forms, had they been able to reflect, could not have imagined us as the next stage of the process.

David, flat on his back, and everyone struggling to

break away from the demands and distractions of life to find You, can take comfort from Haught's vision—God's gift leaves the world free to respond but eventually overcomes whatever non-response that there might be. Nothing tried is ever lost, no joy ever wasted, no love ever in vain. Such truths do not heal the wounds, they are not an excuse for ignoring the suffering of others or accepting injustice. But they are grounds for hope that all is not lost, nothing in fact is lost.

We commit ourselves, he says, to a word of Promise. You are promise. Our life and love is not for an institution or a cause but for Someone who has promised and continues to promise in all the wonders of life. Yet even my response to the lighthouse of Your loving promise is flawed with distractions and the weariness of David on the flat of his back.

In a certain sense, no matter. For reasons that are difficult to understand but surely have to do with Your playful delight in Your creatures, You are happy to settle for even a hint of a response, making up what is lacking by Your own love which, according to Mahon, is given and yet kept.

I wonder how much love there has been in my life? As I write that sentence I realize that there has been a lot, a lot more than I deserve, though I know well that we are not dealing with each other, You and I, in a relationship in which "deserve" counts at all.

My response to all those loves disappoints me, so it must disappoint You even more. For that I'm sorry. With Your help, I'll try to do better.

April 24

MAHON'S POEM is about a deserted garage in Cork, a place which was once home and is no longer but is still remembered by someone, somewhere in the world, as home. Saint Luke tells me about the hundredfold which those who follow him will receive. David in the 122nd Psalm lifts up his eyes to heaven as a servant does to a master and pleads for mercy.

Today I also want to pray for Rich Daley, the new mayor of Chicago, and his family. Protect them from harm, particularly the kids, who might have a hard time of it, and help him to bind up the wounds in Chicago, a place that is as dearly home to so many people as the garage in Cork was to the people in Mahon's poem.

And bring me home safely, please, from Tucson and Europe.

April 25

AGAIN I put off my conversation with You till the end of the day—having risen at 5:30. For that I'm sorry, though I suppose I'm not the first lover who has done that. There seems so much to do these last days in Tucson, so many stimuli from my crowded life.

Overload.

I look forward to coming home from Europe and slowing down for Grand Beach and summer.

And how many times have I thought of that? How often I've come here planning to rest and yet each year here, there is less rest, less enjoyment of warmth and beauty and more time answering the various challenges which cluster around this machine.

Our help is in the name of the Lord who made heaven and earth, David says, bragging about how he and his allies were snatched from the jaws of defeat. One can readily enough, I suppose, translate that into a modern Christian context. I realize that the Psalms are immortal but the need to translate them constantly is a drag.

Anyway, my help is in Your name if I'm going to slow the machine down. Help me to do so. Help me as Saint Luke says today to SEE what is important and what need not be done, not right away.

I've finished Derek Mahon and have gone on to Michael Longley, another Ulster poet. He has a nice metaphor—winter as the season of the sick in heart. Is winter or spring triumphant? I believe that the latter wins but I often seem to live like I fear the victory of the former.

Tomorrow, please God, I'll have time to slow down and think and read and relax before I leave for Chicago and the British Isles.

April 26

ZACHEUS was obviously Your kind of person. So maybe there is hope for me. If Zach's enthusiasm appealed to You, then You must like my enthusiasm too. If that be the case, I can buy what the psalmist says today, "the Lord has done great things for us! We are glad!"

I have often preached about the subject of Your kind

of people, a notion I picked up long ago from an author I don't remember. You seemed to like the enthusiasts— Peter, John, Mary Magdalen, Zacheus, Your mother. Maybe I like that theme because I see myself in that crowd, not, heaven (You should excuse the expression) forfend, in their virtue but only in their enthusiasm. If I try to do too many things it's an excess of a virtue You seem to like. If I lose my enthusiasm, then life becomes pretty empty. Thank You for making me an enthusiast. Help the flames to burn brightly always and protect me from the excesses. You have indeed done great things for me and I am glad!

Michael Longley's poem today is a delicate depiction of two swans engaging in copulation. "This was a marriage and a baptism . . . ./her feathers full of water and her neck/under the water like a bar of light."

A lovely exercise in the pathetic fallacy. Last night I saw two doves in their nest near my front door, their bodies pressed together in what we humans interpret spontaneously as affection. More pathetic fallacy. Neither the doves nor the swans feel love as we do. We read our emotions and our reactions into their behavior.

Yet, for someone who believes in sacramentality, any bonding behavior can be interpreted as a hint of Your binding Yourself to us. So we bring the swans and the doves in through the back door. We indeed read our emotions into them but we can do that legitimately because Your emotions are revealed through them—and, more powerfully if more problematically, through us.

The doves (there's a second pair on the back of the house, I'm surrounded by love this year!) are genetically programmed to huddle together at night. We have a highly plastic propensity to do the same thing (literally or figuratively) but we can resist that propensity. Our love is more like Yours because it is free. The doves have no choice. We do.

We can refuse to be sacraments.

Enthusiasm and love coexist, in my life anyway, uneasily. Projects tend to get in the way of people. And when I'm tired from the projects the people who, like David's enemies, assault me, stir up the same response as they did in David. Let's smite them!

Not a very good sacramental response, is it?

I'm sorry. Help me to balance love and enthusiasm and not to become so weary that I become preoccupied with smiting.

Tomorrow is the last day of class. I'll be up late correcting papers. Then back to Chicago and on to Europe. I propose to continue this journal on my Toshiba during the trip.

April 27

LADY WISDOM,

9:02 in the morning. I'm finally starting this journal when I should.

Saint Luke tells me today the parable of the talents and David warns me that unless the Lord builds the house they labor in vain who build it. Michael Longley describes a tinker's caravan—horse-drawn wagon—"A rickety chimney suggests/the diminutive stove/children perhaps, the pots and pans adding up to love."

So much love, everywhere cast about, profligate like

the sands of the desert, drops of water in the ocean, molecules of air. Never perfect, always transient, forever doomed to be defeated by sickness, age, and death. And yet implacable, beyond defeat, discouragement, and disillusion.

Against such a background I must reflect on the parable of talents, another story of the demand of Jesus for enthusiasm. Like the Zacheus story, the talent parable appeals to me. I've always felt that I've worked with the talents given me for God and Church by intent, but not always completely so in execution. Sometimes, I fear, I have built the house by myself without Your help.

And yet, Lady Wisdom, if I am to believe the stories You tell about Yourself, You work on the house even when I don't pay any attention to You and when I try my best to pretend that You are not there. All You expect of me is that I occasionally acknowledge Your presence and Your help.

So I do that today: the talents with which I try to build my house, my house of love like the gypsy's wagon, are sustained and supported by Your loving presence. Without You they are worthless even for short run selfishness.

Help me to remember that and to grow in loving trust.

April 28

7:00 AM

Last day in Tucson. Fourteen weeks since I came and it seems like only yesterday. The semester was so badly cut up by trips back and forth that it never seemed to start. I must re-evaluate this segment of my life, as I have said before many times. I had planned to rest and relax here and did practically none of either. I am much more tired now than I was at the beginning of the semester.

It's hard to leave, hard to end the class which was great fun, hard to say goodby to friends, hard to close up the house, pull all the electric cords, clean out the fridge, turn off the pool. Depressing work at best and when I'm tired and feel under assault, even more depressing.

April 30

THE priesthood is in terrible shape. Six young priests left because they did want to be priests but they did not want to be celibates. Well, in the present order of things they don't want to be priests. I don't mind their departure, but I am upset by the folk hero status which has been consistently awarded to those who leave, as though they are the wave of the future and we who remain somehow represent the past.

Well, I pray for them too and for all priests. Help me to be the priest You want me to be, a much better one than I am now and to make good use of the opportunities and challenges You have put in my life.

Even this trip, which I don't want to take—no way.

This afternoon, while relaxing before the flight, I saw the new film, *Field of Dreams,* a delicate masterpiece of a morality play about heaven and purgatory and baseball. I saw Your hand in it all the way, a sermon designed to reveal not only the ways of God but Her playfulness.

There was not a dry eye in the 900 Theatre (first time there) when Kevin Kostner played catch with his father as a young man. We'll be using that before the summer is over.

Time now for the last preparations before O'Hare. Take care of me and bring me back safe and as relaxed as I can be after a trip.

Dublin, May 3

YOU know, even if everyone else doesn't, that I had already written two paragraphs of prayer and that my lap-top went haywire and lost them.

I have been doing much reflecting on Ireland since I've been here, prayerful reflection I hope. Too bad the people don't realize how unique and special they are—wit, language, philosophy. Somehow they have survived the tragedy of all the years with grace and style—a reflection of You. If there is a sacramental people anywhere in the world it is the Irish, and there is some of it left in us Irish Americans too. For which both peoples must be grateful to You.

We more than they because we are free enough of the self-hatred to see it.

It's a silly dream, but I'd like to spend a month or so here each year, learning more and becoming more part of the tradition, as if I didn't have enough else to do.

Too short an entry. Computer trouble eight or nine times. I love You more than all the others. Help me to love You even more in this country where Your love is specially revealed.

Andrew Greeley

May 6, Bishop's House, Galway

I CAME as close as I'm ever likely to come to a mystical experience yesterday on a mountaintop in Connemara. I said my thirty-fifth anniversary Mass in a little shrine called Kileen Phodraig where You have been worshipped in various forms since the time of Abraham. My friend Mihail McGreal has rebuilt the shrine as a pilgrimage site and he insisted that I make the pilgrimage, which I did with as much grace as possible. Then when I had reached the top (not winded, thanks to Your insistence that I swim) and began to say Mass overlooking the mountains and the moors and the bays, I felt continuity with all the priests who had ever said Mass there and all the people who had ever worshipped You there and of course with You who have made me a priest to serve the descendents of those who came to the nineteenth century "patterns" there (and those festivals complete with vast amounts of poteen, were no better than they had to be) and with You who have made me a priest to serve those people.

On this the day after my thirty-fifth anniversary, I thank You again.

I thought often yesterday that thirty-five years ago, on the coldest May 5 in history, I would not have dreamed in my wildest moments that I'd be driving around Ireland with as gifted a character as Mihail, much less that I would have become what I have become in the priesthood. I am grateful for the graces which have drawn me in the direction I have traveled and sad only that I have not responded as gracefully as I might have. I'm especially sorry for the anger and the disillusion and the weariness and the discouragement, especially the last two which are to some extent under my control.

Today, somehow (and maybe it's the sun shining down on Galway Bay!) I feel renewed and reinvigorated, while yesterday I felt under great pressure—nothing like a ten-hour sleep to improve hope, is there?

Maybe when I get home to Grand Beach I can begin to feel that way every day. At any rate, thanks to You, this spiritual journal will force me to look over the words I've written and the promises I've made and try to honor them.

May 15, Grand Beach

TEN DAYS without an entry. I know You know the reason why and continue to love me regardless. I must mention it to You for my sake and not Yours.

The trip caught me up both in fatigue and in an incredibly full schedule and then terrible jet lag on return, three nights without sleeping. A human lover would forgive my weariness, so all the more would You. I'm sorry that I let myself become so exhausted.

I came up here yesterday, as You know, and am beginning to recover. I have one more trip on Thursday and then it's over. Next week in Chicago touching bases with people and then here for most of the summer. I can already feel the relaxation beginning—its palpable as soon as I drive in the gate.

More later when I return to my spiritual reading and am able to relax.

May 17

I'M STILL wandering around in a fog caused by jet lag, a cold, and sudden bursts of compulsive energy which yesterday caught me up in research that I really shouldn't have begun.

However, I am slowly coming back to normal in the glorious May weather here at Grand Beach, for both of which I am grateful. I shall seek shelter under Yahweh's wings, as the psalm says today. I'll need a lot of extra shelter while I try to wind down.

I've been reading new Irish fiction and plays—McGuinness and Banville—and while I'm not yet restored enough to cope with their themes, they are obsessed with death and aging. And also, Irish-like, with the salvation of the ordinary. It is in the ordinary that I must find You and regeneration in the next few weeks. Please help me.

May 20

I KNOW it's beginning to sound like a worn out record, but I'm still dead tired—too much travel, too little food, too little rest, maybe too much exercise, surely too much work.

I'm sorry for having overdone it in all these areas. When I see my confessor next week I'll try to renew the strength of my relationship with You and the Church and seek new vitality from this renewal. I've never needed rest and refreshment so much in all my life. Confession won't do it all but it will be a useful symbolic help.

The psalm today says I almost stumbled. Right! The stumble of which the poet speaks is a loss of faith, not theoretical faith, he is anything but theoretical, but practical faith, the faith that I don't have to do everything, that I should be content with the widow's mite about which I read in Saint Luke today. I am more than the widow but still, from the point of view of eternity, not much more. I don't have to save the Church by myself (as someone once suggested rather nastily when introducing me).

Oddly enough, despite my weariness I am doing my best work ever, running on autopilot. Not worth it.

The poems I read today, Longley and Your man Seamus, were both about fathers. They made me think of my own father, such a distant man after forty-two years, distant even then. A model of integrity and wit and industry and yet so far away from me. Who was he really? Perhaps I can learn when we meet again. As far as I can see, the only differences between us are that he died earlier because he smoked too much and he was wiped out by a depression.

I still fear the latter more than the former.

Strange.

And very Irish, huh?

May 21, Trinity Sunday

THIS is the first day since I left Tucson that I feel reasonably good, not exhausted, not sick, not depressed. I marvel at the resiliency of the human organism. How quickly a good night's sleep and a little relaxation restores our energy and our vigor—and our false sense of invulnerability.

The psalmist says today that he acted like a fool, Saint Luke warns us of the signs represented by the fig tree (the boy seems to have confused that parable beyond recognition) and Seamus Heaney celebrates the ordinary. A true sacramental poet, Your man Seamus. I am always a fool when I lose my sense of wonder and awe over Your presence in the ordinary, the everyday. I, especially, who sing the wonders of the Catholic sacramental imagination and of the Irish Catholic version of it.

It's a fantastic May day in Chicago, blue sky, clear air, the city and the lake out my windows glowing in the morning sunlight. How can I not believe in You and trust You on a day like this?

I am, as You perceive, coming up for air, a resurrection of a sort. I feel euphoric—and also charged up again, which is all right up to a point, anyway. But it is only a tentative resurrection, one that will have to last a lot longer if I am going to be truly sensitive as I should to the sacramentality of the ordinary.

May 23

I'VE MADE a new discovery: nothing, as John Shea has told me, is ever lost in the mind of God. Hence I do not have to redo my last two entries which were lost in the mind of Microsoft Word! Neat. The computer may forget but You don't.

For the first time it is not necessary to retype something that is lost. Wonderful!

May 24

SEAMUS HEANEY'S poem today is a love poem, about a healing reconciliation with his weeping wife (I think that's what is about, with Your man Seamus one can never be absolutely certain). It's a wonderful poem, profoundly erotic and religious at the same time. In a world where there is such love and love renewal there must be hope. There has to be goodness and grounds for life. Nothing like that is ever lost in the mind of God, the process people say, and I believe that, I cling to it with all my strength. There is nothing else to cling to, is there?

Waiting in the dentist's chair this morning, nineteen stories above Michigan Avenue, I noticed a spider spinning her web. Grandmother spider holding the world together, as the Native American folk tales would say. A superb example of the profligate nature of life, reasserting itself in the most improbable places every spring. There is a poem in that little scene and I'll write it when I get to Grand Beach.

As today continues—and a mad busy day it will be—help me to remember Grandma spider and love renewed.

May 26

FRIDAY, the beginning of the Memorial Day weekend and the real beginning of summer, even if the weather is often too cold on this day. I'm heading for Grand Beach tonight, You being willing, and what may be the most important summer of my life, the summer in which I truly slow down. Help me to honor all my good resolutions.

I slept for two hours yesterday afternoon and got rid of the headache. Again I reflect on how civilized was the custom of the afternoon nap. Winston Churchill did it, why shouldn't everyone!

Anyway, Seamus writes a beautiful poem about love manifested in the baking of bread for a family—another example of his powerful, powerful instinct about the sacramentality of the ordinary. In Luke, Jesus has his disciples prepare for the Paschal supper and David's psalm celebrates (in our old class motto) how good it is for brothers to dwell together in unity, something the class never did (and God rest Tom Crawford who made that the class motto). Your message ought to be coming through loud and clear for me — search for Yourself in the ordinary world. At Grand Beach this summer, with Your help, I'll do just that.

May 27

TODAY is perfect for the beginning of summer, a bit cool perhaps, but then Memorial weekend ought not to be too warm in the midwest, ought it? The village hums with activity, just as I described it in *Rite of Spring.* Flowers spring up everywhere as folk scurry about to do their Memorial Day planting. New Buffalo swarms with people. Lawn furniture, my own included, a little worse for the winter wear, appears at poolside and on decks. Cruisers sweep by on the lake, an occasional catamaran races along the shore. The trees are now in full bloom and the flowering trees at their best.

In Luke, talk at the last supper about betraying Jesus. We all do it, of course. Judas is everyone.

On this lovely day with the promise of summer ahead do not let me deceive myself about the dark side of life. But also impress ever more deeply on my soul that spring and summer are the ultimate and not the penultimate symbols.

MAY 28

GRACIOUS LORD,

In Patrick O'Connor's book of prayers there is one I read today from Madagascar which asks the earth for mercy: "It is upon thee that I dwell. It's thou that gives to me my food and the water I drink, it is thou that givest me my clothes. Be merciful toward me, O Earth!"

Today, with summer oozing out all over the place, I should realize again that earth is a sacrament of You— either that or an absurd deception and that is intolerable. Even if it is a deception, by my very saying that I imply a deceiver which, of course, is what You are not.

May 29, Memorial Day

IN addition to the other books I am reading and on which I'm trying to reflect, I have come upon Enda Mac-Donough's book of prayers and poems. The poem today is about emptiness, the absence, the vacuum which You do not deign to abhor.

Interesting image. I wonder if I am capable of it. Or is my life too hectic, too busy, to encounter, save in my dreams, terror and emptiness. When I slow down in the days, do not the dreams of terror come again at night? Last night I was once again in my alternative archdiocese, worrying about chimed clocks and the passage of time. Perhaps there is a poem here, too, for this gloomy Memorial Day, a day to commemorate the gloom of all the fine young men who died in foolish wars. May there not be any others.

I must reflect often this summer on such things and search for a sense of emptiness and of fullness.

Also I must thank You for making my sensibility what it is and not someone else's.

May 30

THE first day of really hot summer weather, reassuring and rehabilitating by itself.

Enda turns to Australian poetry today, a fellow named McAuley, who sees in the naming of things a hint of resurrection, the triumph of mind over pure matter. It's a nice way to restate the principle of sacramentality, a communication of meaning and minds through creation, a sense of the God-like presence in us. I like that. It points at the mystery of meaning, the utter improbability of the universe being meaningless. The neat thing about the argument is that the very act of giving meaning to the smallest of realities by naming it points to the ultimate cosmic

question. Then it circles back to Saint Luke in the Garden
of Olives and David's simple faith in the early psalms
I'm reading now.

I don't have much trouble accepting the mystery of
meaning—creation does mean something. My difficulty
is slowing down enough to encounter the mystery in
daily life. Which is why the best spiritual thing I can do
this summer is to write poetry, in other words to explore
the sacramentality of Your creation—Your presence in
the world.

I have to make time to do that, after I clean up the last
pile of revisions which wait on my desk.

The principle of sacramentality, meaning in creation,
brings me back to David who saw You puffing around
in the sky in a thunderstorm, one of which is coming
across the lake at this moment. My interpretation may
be a little different than his, but not as much as I sometimes think when I read his elementary poetry. David
and McAuley worked on the same fundamental insight:
God is everywhere, both mystery and illumination.

June 8

I NOTE that in Patrick's book of prayers the Africans
are very much into barter with You. One of them even
says after a sacrifice that now "I have bought You."
Others are furious that they have made the sacrifices and
You have not responded to them. The psalmist sometimes edges dangerously close to similar sentiments. But
then don't we all. You have made it clear through the
prophets and through Jesus that You don't accept such

an approach and that You are not for sale. One does not barter with Lady Wisdom. No way. Yet some of it is Your own fault, You must admit. Your ways not being our ways and Your behavior not predictable, You invite the magical approach. So much of the superstitious end of Catholicism (nine as a magic number) and the private revelation aspect (the current disturbance in Croatia) are the result of our need to be certain that You are on our side.

Your word is not enough, You see. It's not that we don't believe You. It's rather that we're not sure You'll remember or that You'll adjust Your ways to our ways. Therefore we try if not exactly to buy You, then to add a little more certainty to our relationships with You.

You say that all You want is love and trust in return. That's asking a lot. Most folks in the course of human history don't think that whatever is responsible for the cosmos is of that sort at all.

You insist that You are and I'm not prepared to disagree. Yet I want You to admit that it's easier to deal with a negotiator than with a lover.

Alane Rollins puts it nicely in one of her poems which I am currently reading: our vocation is not to despair over despair—a minimalism perhaps but still not bad.

June 9

Patrick Kavanaugh's poem today is about women as a sign of God, a nice anticipation of feminist theology, as Enda says in his commentary. How much trouble would have been avoided in the long history of Catholicism if this insight, incarnated in the Mary symbol, had been able to overcome Augustine's guilt feelings. If the relationship between men and women is flawed today, much of the reason surely is the persistence of inequality in the relationship. Men and women are too busy fighting one another for power in their intimacies (quite apart from feminist ideology which is almost irrelevant to the prennial war between the sexes) to enjoy one another, to revel in the differences and the complementarities.

Fine for a celibate to say who doesn't have to live in the intimate friction of the love/conflict which exists between physical lovers. Unlike a lot of my classmates who have married, I doubt that I would be all that good in such a friction—not that they are either; only they think they are.

Most men are not good at it. Neither are most women.

Yet no one wants to write sexual difference off, either.

Anyway, thank You for the differences and for the revelation of Yourself in them. Help me to be more sensitive to what I can learn about You from them.

Gray weather today. Summer postponed. I'm about ready to start writing my own poetry.

June 11

TEN O'CLOCK on Sunday night and at last I get to You, not indeed as reflective and refreshing interlude, which is what my prayer ought to be, but as a final obligation on a day of rest which filled up with obligations, many of which forced me back to this machine when I did not want to look at it. I have begun to hate the computer and resent the work I must do on it, even typing out letters and addressing envelopes. Will the nuisance tasks ever end, I find myself asking.

The answer is that no they won't and I must learn not to resent them. Just now, however, they are intruding on my time of rest and reflection and eating into my vacation, already one-sixth over.

June 12

MONDAY and the rains have returned. You have clearly heard the farmers' prayers. The drought is gone from much of the middle west—though those who insist there is a greenhouse effect are upset that this summer so far isn't as hot as they say it should be.

If it would be all the same to You, I'd like some consisent nice weather.

Which is as good a way as any to begin the subject of prayers of petition.

I was struck by some of the African prayers I have been reading in Patrick's book. They are often quite beautiful, the prayer of a chief on the occasion of his daughter's engagement, for example. On the other hand the prayers for victory in time of war or for successful cattle raids are harsh and to me offensive—even if we did pray for victory in our wars. So many of their prayers and our prayers, too, sound like barter. You are the major general in charge of strategy, the vice president in charge of good weather, the minister for supernatural affairs. We do our part for You and You are expected to live up to the contract and do Your part for us.

Nice and neat and well ordered. And magical. And profoundly unchristian. Yet in the gospel I read today Your son accepts the prayer of the good thief.

I am suspicious of the prayer style of many of us; it does not seem to recognize either Your freedom or Your mystery or Your refusal to interfere in natural processes. Make my wife (or mother) better for example. Don't take her away with cancer. How can one not pray that way? Yet what good does the prayer do? Does one really expect it to cure her? Is it possible that sufficient prayers do modify the biological environment for a sick person or perhaps the psychological environment and thus strengthen the will to live?

Can our prayer interfere in the ordinary natural processes?

Can our prayer, for example, change the viciousness of the current Chinese leadership?

I am particularly offended by those enthusiasts who rush off to Serbia to change their rosaries into gold by attending a certain shrine. That's magic for sure.

Yet we must pray, must we not? Even the African cattle raiders are praying for life. We pray, as I tell people, because we need to pray not because You need to hear our prayers and not because that will change the process of nature or history, not because we expect special miraculous intervention. They don't always listen to me. Some of them do expect special miraculous intervention, even sophisticated college-educated people, whose belief in priest faith healers is no different from the Africans' in Patrick's prayer book.

The problem is insoluble ultimately because it goes to the heart of Your mystery, of who and what You are and why You work the way You do, which none of us can even begin to understand. We pray because we must pray, we pray because we need You and depend upon You, we pray because we believe that somehow prayers do enter into Your calculus though not in a magical fashion, we pray as Your son did that Your will, but not ours, be done.

Just the same we would rather like it if Your will, manifested through the natural and providential calculus we do not understand, was not all that different from our will.

I'd like nice weather, in other words, if You don't mind.

And I'll offer my prayers of petition with more insistence (as Your son said we should) in the days to come. At least I will try to.

June 13

MORE rain and cold. Summer may never come.

The poem in Enda's book hit me hard—Eavan Boland's reflection on Renoir's "Girlhood." The poet gazes at the two kids as they "face the future. If they only knew!"

For, the poet observes, the "horizon is the past and all they look forward to is memory."

Brrr!

There is something terribly appealing about a young girl and her dreams and hopes—the time when, as someone has said, she likes to read and maybe even write poetry. Their male counterparts never develop (or perhaps never reveal) the sensitivity, the openness, the wonder that so many early and middle teen girls seem to possess in superabundance.

This hope, alas the poet and Renoir are right, will turn into memory of the time of hope which will be seen as a glorious if deceptive era in life. In my own dismal observation the wonder ends in the first semester of the first year of college, the time when they begin, as their mothers and often their older sisters tell them, to settle down and learn what life is really like.

They learn soon enough: men are brutes, husbands are insensitive, children are ungrateful, the body is frail, life is short, frustration and unhappiness blight much of it. And we are all born to die.

I've watched several generations now go through this interlude which I believe to be sacramental. Needless to say I have not been able to protect any of them from hope turning into memory, and usually bittersweet memory. Now, like their mothers, they do all they can to free their daughters from illusion, to soften, they would say, the future disappointments of life.

Somehow it seems a terrible waste. Why do You plant so much hope if it is not going to flower but rather turn to bitter seed? I don't doubt that You know what You are doing, yet this does seem to be a pathetic sacrament.

You may well argue that the hope of the young, espe-cially of young women, is indeed a sacrament and that it presages resurrection and transcendence. Who am I to doubt that? I guess the church fails to teach this strongly enough, we are too busy warning them about how evil their bodies are. Hope is the sacrament, disillusion is not. I believe that, but sometimes it's hard to really believe it when You see disillusion triumphing over hope in people You have come to love.

One must leave them free to their own disillusion, to their own contempt for their memories and hope that such contempt may, in a kind of second naivete, be replaced by stronger and more experienced hope.

It ain't easy, but as my all-time favorite fictional young woman, Noele Farrell, puts it, resurrection isn't supposed to be easy.

June 15

HEAVY, heavy literary consumption the last couple of days—Beuchner's *Brendan, Bright Lights/Big City* on the screen. Both are concerned with, indeed obsessed with death. I conclude from experiencing them that it is a mistake to want anything too much; Michael Fox in the film wants his wife back; Brendan wants to find the multi-colored lands. Wanting too strongly is a revolt against death.

Yet we pray for what we want, to continue that reflection. Jesus prayed in the Garden and on the cross, even if he represented a God who wanted to become like us so that he could face death like we do.

Maybe I don't fear death enough. Maybe I repressed it with a combination of good health (for which I am grateful) and energy. Or maybe that's the way to live. Brendan did surely. Maybe I want too much. Or maybe I don't want enough.

It is human to want, human to ask, human to fear death. To deny any of these things, even in the name of sanctity is to refuse to be human. Repression is escape from mature responsiblity. But how does one want and yet not want too much? Like everything else in life that matters, it is tricky. The temptation of religious enthusiasm is to make things simple, in this case to repress, to detach oneself. That's fine if you're a Hindu, but it won't do if you're a Catholic living in a sacramental world.

So I must be content to want, to ask, to fear, and to laugh with faith.

Help me to do that. Help me to do it better than I have before.

June 20

LAST day of spring, a cold, gray, and disappointing spring, appropriately enough ending in a fog. Yet I have a wonderful spring/summer quote from Alane Rollings on which to ponder today: "When You sit in the sun, You don't need proof of it."

Right! I suppose there's no better argument for You than that. When You exist in the marvels of creation, You hardly need proof for a Marvelous Creator. It's only when You retreat from the marvels and into the mind that doubts emerge. Since we are creatures with mind, such retreats are inevitable, but not definitive.

The trick is to trust in that first instinct for the marvelous, no easy task, the hint of benignity, the aura of promise, the envelope of grace which seems to be there on the rim of our vision.

Ken Woodward was on the phone this morning talking about prayer and a possible article on prayer. It set me thinking about that subject again. We are fated to pray, programmed to pray, doomed to pray. It is built into our nature as creatures who reflect on their own mortality and who all see the traces of hope out on the rim. Even if we deny the traces out there we still pray in moments of crisis because there is nothing else to do.

To whom it may concern?

One could do worse.

My own propensity not to bother You with my petitions is a sign in its own way of a weakness of faith—faith in Your love for me, in Your desire to hear from me, even in Your need to hear from me.

If we are right about the pathos of God then You want to hear from me. A good enough reason for praying, even with my petitions. They are acts of love and not requests for favors.

I must turn in my catalogue of requests every day. DeLubac was right—we are only fully human when the light of the divinity is reflected in a face upturned in prayer.

June 21

MIDSUMMER'S DAY, the summer solstice, the longest day of the year, Saint John's night—whatever. As if to celebrate the day, You sent summer, nice summer, not hot dry or hot humid summer, but nice middle eighties with a light breeze summer. For which many thanks.

I was reading yesterday Fred Wolf's book about parallel universes. I kind of agree with the critics who think this theory is nothing more than a foolish construct to make sense of quantum theory and of the odd impact an observer has on quantum mechanics. They have bumped up against mystery, possibly with a capital M, and are plainly confused—brilliant, ingenious, and confused.

If You were the kind that delights in mystifying people—and I think You are—You must have great fun with the quantum game. I can see no other reason for making the cosmos that way, indeed making it so that Wolf will propose with a perfectly straight face that we need a universe for every particle that exists, something like ten to the hundredth power cosmoses.

For all I know there may be that many or even more. What is funny, however, is that a theory can drive a reasonable man to postulate the necessity for that many.

All of which brings me back to the subject of prayer about which I have been pondering these days. How can someone so busy about so many complex issues give a hoot about whether Saint John's night is lovely or not. There are automatic laws dealing, as I gather now, with the behavior of the jet stream, which arrange such matters.

Yet You are a lover and all Your gifts, even those indirectly given (if one can say that when You are at work) are gifts of love which should be acknowledged and treasured—even when the mechanics of Your love are even more baffling than quantum mechanics.

Help me to be sensitive to the gifts that lurk everywhere—like the sun for which we need no proof when we bask in its light.

Andrew Greeley

June 27

WE'RE different today. I read a prayer in Patrick's book from a primitive people which sounds much like a psalm—though more beautiful than most of them. Humans stand at the head of creation, the prayer says, alone, distinct from all the other animals and isolated in the responsibility which comes from that distinction. They need God to be their companion. Very nice.

Last night I read Bob Lauder's book on Ingmar Bergman and discovered the very opposite and very modern attitude, the fear of being alone, the decision that one is alone, the resolution that, despite being alone, one can love and thus give life meaning.

Bergman is satisfied with that decision. Alane Rollings is less satisfied with a similar decision. They represent the modern quest for God, perhaps no more agonized than that of the psalmist or the poet in Patrick's book, (a Yakut I find in checking the book). Maybe the more "primitive" people had the same doubts we do and lacked the rhetoric to express it. Maybe their bright, almost arrogant, confidence covered up the same hesitations and doubts. Maybe all we have done is to learn how to express our doubts honestly.

Bergman, Lutheran that he is and captive of the dialectical imagination, cannot see love as a sacrament of God, though in fact that's what it plays even in his films, a hint of purpose and affection, a suggestion of the protecting "umwelt." Maybe the God he no longer worries about wasn't a God worth worrying about. Maybe the driving force of the universe as revealed in human love is a God worth worrying about even though Bergman cannot call that force God.

If there is love then there must be a Lover, right? You, in other words. Maybe the end of the Reformation or, perhaps better, the end of the Augustinian component of Christianity will come about because it has not the possibility of using that metaphor. Not that we have made much better use of it.

Anyway . . . Ricoeur is right, we are beyond the first naivete in which maybe the psalmist and the Yakut poet lived. Most of us are caught in the critical interlude and have yet to reach to the second naivete—most of the time.

I don't doubt You. I'm sure You're there. I'm sure that You're Love. I'm sure that human love is a revelation of You. Only I don't always live that way. Help me to do better.

Help me also to begin this vacation. Almost the end of June and I'm still somehow catching up.

June 28

AS I ponder the different style with which we moderns and our predecessors (a better word than primitives, is it not?) reflect about You and pray to You, I think the basic question is finally whether we can trust You. When moderns like Bergman decide that You don't exist or that the question is irrelevant or that they have headaches from pondering the issue and don't want to think about it anymore, they are not behaving all that differently from our predecessors when they plead with You to remember the promises You made to them. Our manner of dealing with this issue is more reflective and more agonized because we have the vocabulary to behave in that fashion, to struggle in the no-person's-land between the two naivetes. Our unease however is not all that different, save perhaps that articulated unease may be more poignant than unarticulated unease.

The data, as I have often said and written, are ambiguous. There are some reasons to believe in graciousness and other reasons to doubt it. The earlier human lamenting over his crops and the more modern one pondering evil and suffering see the latter reasons. Yet a harvest or a needed rain or the birth of a child or a beautiful day or human love (pace Bergman) are always there to tell the other side of the story.

I have argued with my friend Al Bergesen that Your message is loud and clear: consider for example this incredibly lovely early summer morning. I must admit, however, that sometimes it seems less loud and less clear. Bergman deciding that You don't exist or don't care and the predecessors offering more sacrifices to get Your attention are focusing on other data than this morning. But to make their decisions on the basis of these data they have to ignore the conflicting evidence or, in the case of Bergman, abort the discussion by opting for human love without asking the fundamental question of why there is human love.

In other words, the human species is probably temperamentally and possibly biologically incapable of rejecting graciousness. Hence we live poised on a knife edge and able to remove ourself from the edge only by denying one or the other sets of data. Only those who assert both and admit that they cannot give up, no matter how hard they try, the evidence of loveliness like this morning are true to reality.

Why You would arrange things this way baffles me, as it has baffled everyone else. At any rate, help me to stay on the knife's edge, rejoicing in the grace of a morning like this.

June 29

AS I continue to pray about prayer I reflect on the phenomenon of Your working (usually) through secondary causes. I leave aside the issue of miracles, of whether they are in fact violations of the ordinary laws of nature (of quantum mechanics?) I don't doubt that You can suspend such laws. I'm not sure that You do and I am sure that You don't do it very often. In the normal course of events You work through the usual processes of the universe. Take the case of my recently missing wallet which I must have knocked out of the car when I picked John up for skiing on Sunday. My visitors Sunday instituted prayers to Saint Anthony. I searched in vain, using self-hypnosis to recall the events of the morning.

Yesterday the kids who cut the lawns brought it back to me, having found it in some bushes. Would I have recovered it without my friends' prayers? Ah, that's the question, isn't it? I called them and thanked them in any case. But without their prayers, the kids would have found the wallet anyhow, would they not? And they would have delivered it to me anyhow, would they not?

Huh?

I'm not sure, to tell the truth. Maybe I've been reading

Andrew Greeley

too much lately about quantum dynamics. We live in an uncertain, problematic, oddly (one might almost say humorously) shaped cosmos. Who knows how it ultimately works. Moreover who knows how You work through secondary causes?

The Navajo Thunderbird prayer I read this morning in Patrick's book assumes Your direct responsibility for everything that happens. So did my friends who prayed for the lost wallet. So do those who are angry at You for problems in their life for which they are not responsible—suffering, sickness, death. So did King David or whoever wrote those psalms.

I guess there are two extremes to be avoided (listen to me as an Aristotelian!). First, one rejects the vulgar notion of miracles happening at every turn (as those who come back from Yugoslavia with golden rosaries would persuade us) and on the other hand, one also rejects the notion of that Your normal mode of working through secondary causes makes prayer unnecessary. One must be neither superstitious nor materialist. One must pray with the faith of my Sunday visitors—and the sense of intimacy with You that such prayer represents—and with the sophistication of those who realize that You do not directly intervene in the ordinary processes of the cosmos which You have set in motion and whose (messy and mysterious?) dynamics You have established.

That doesn't solve much, especially since the word "directly" implies a metaphysics which may have nothing to do with either You or a quantum universe. It's also a nice cop out. But then when one deals with Mystery one needs an escape hatch.

Bottom line: I should have prayed more for the wallet. In any event thank You for its return.

June 30

THE last day of June, a perfect time to meditate on the transiency of life and the inevitability of death. One less June in my life, only two months away from one less summer. Only a few summers left at the most.

I don't think much about death, unlike some of my friends who are endlessly haunted and troubled by it. On the whole, I believe that living for the present moment and trusting in You for the final moments is the only sensible way to cope with life. On the other hand that's easy when You have never had any major physical sufferings in life. And perhaps I miss an important tragic dimension of life by not paying more attention to death and to my own death. One of the valid criticisms of my novels is that they lack a sense of the tragic (unlike Graham Greene). Fair enough, though one should be true to one's own sensibility. Nonetheless, I ought to reflect more on death and on my death, if only to prepare more for it and to give more perspective to my life.

Perhaps it will also help me to slow down. I'm juggling too many things a third of the way through the summer. Maybe that's part of my life. Right now I'm forgetting and losing things because I'm trying to do too much— everything is too closely scheduled.

Maybe that's part of my sensibility too. It makes prayer difficult however.

As You well know. Help me to pray better. It's nine now, I'm about to leave the house to waterski. I've been going at breakneck speed trying to get things done before I leave and am already stressed out, as the kids say. No good.

July 4

WELL, I made it to the beach yesterday, for the first time this summer. What kind of a vacation is this, where I can't get away from the phone and the machines long enough to make it to the beach? What is the point of having a house on the beach if You don't use the beach?

This is not the first summer in which the demands of work and the demands of hospitality have worn me out and destroyed the summer rest before it could begin. Help me not to do it again. You note that not only have I not had time to relax the last couple of days, I haven't had much time to pray either. I'm usually frazzled even before I leave the house to ski and counting the minutes as I ski so that I can get back and cope with responsibilities.

That's quite mad, isn't it?

And it will be another ten days before the burdens of responsibility and hospitality are adequately discharged. Dear God, help to me relax anyway. Help me to read, reflect, pray, write poetry, all those good things which I want to do and You want me to do.

July 5

NOT a bad day to think about death actually. My body is a wreck, partly from a solid week of water skiing, and partly from a spill I took walking down the steps to the beach last night, and myself perfectly sober, as the Irish would say. One can pretend to immorality but such pretenses begin to fail when the body won't quite do this year what it did last year or ten years ago. I don't feel old. But there are not all that many summers of water skiing or Grand Beach left.

Three people in the community dying of cancer, all bravely, all tragically. There are no good ways of dying, I guess. I wouldn't want to have to choose, quick and painless, slow and painless with a chance to say good by, slow and painful in a hospital with the collapse of all human dignity? None very nice, not really.

But one of them is as certain for me as it was for Jesus, as it is for everyone, as it is for the three women in the community. Some day my obituary will appear, perhaps in the not too distant future. It will doubtless say something about "steamy" novels, a phrase they can't give up. Maybe about the three homes too. Then after a while I will be gone and forgotten. Some will mourn me and some will celebrate my death, foolishly, because theirs is not so far off either. That will be that. I will have lived a brief time, done a few things and then will disappear. Vanity of vanities and all is vanity!

One must live both preparing for death and refusing to let death interfere with life. Not easy. One of the reasons, I suspect, for the depression which seems to underlie much of what I do now is that I am at a pre-conscious level more aware of death than I am at the conscious level. I am depressed at the thought of dying, a reasonable enough grounds for depression, it seems to me!

In Paul to the Philippians this morning there is a cry of triumph in the ardor of his work for Jesus. I have worked hard, heaven knows. I hope for Jesus, yet it is so hard to sort out what one does for God and for self. As death draws closer help me to be clear about the difference between those goals, the need of both, the paramount importance of the former.

July 7

I MUST drive to Chicago. Life slips away on such rides. There'll be less of them in my life ahead than there have already been. So much death all around, I pray for those who are dying, pray for myself, pray for all of us who begin to die the day we are born. I have lived to see my teenagers have teenagers. It is unlikely that I will live to see their teenagers. So what?

But then so what for all my other efforts, successes and failures, ephemeral at their most successful, irrelevant at their worst failures. Still I continue to work, to dream, to plan, to drive to Chicago—why? Because You do what You can do while You can do it and that it is what our life here on earth should mean between the two oblivions.

Or is that too pessimistic? Paul—or whoever—in the passage of Colossians that I read today, says the whole world is bearing fruit. I do not want to get caught up in meditation on human history and God's history because that is a headache-producing mystery. Yet I do believe that the world bears fruit and continues to bear fruit and that it would bear more fruit if only we who are Your followers would be generous and open-minded enough to permit it.

Yet in working for the bearing of fruit, as I have tried to do during my life, we must not forget that You give the increase and that in our work we should keep our eyes on the ultimate goals.

There would be more fruit then.

July 8

I CONTINUE to find myself rushed. No real relaxation or recollection yet. I did make it to the beach for about a half hour yesterday. It's problematic that I will do so today. Even though my guests, tragically, will not come this weekend, going slow seems to elude me. I rush through life trying to avoid death, trying to assert my own immortality through work and achievement when most of what I do is either a waste of time or not worth that much.

Yet what I do is what I am supposed to do. I need little persuasion of that. Nor can I do anything about the four phone calls before I got out of the house yesterday morning at 8:30, three of them as I was going out the door. Who will they phone when I am dead?

I must put up with that. I also must escape earlier to the beach today. Help me to slow down.

July 9

THIS MORNING I read Enda MacDonagh on death, the last chapter of his fine book. It kind of reminded me of Jack Shea's story about the Good Theologian who is so busy trying to develop a theological method and explanation for the plight of the injured man that he had no time to help him. Enda addresses himself to such human catastrophes as Auchswitz and AIDS and Hiroshima as though they add a new dimension to the death problem. This is typical theological reflection these days, I fear. It rails and protests and shouts as though somehow the intolerability of AIDS (for example) somehow proves the social injustice of death. Identifying with the victim seems the ultimate protest against it. No raging against the drunken drivers who kill more people than does AIDS and with human responsibility. No raging against the death of a single little kid killed by a drunken driver, or a drunken parent.

I'm sorry, and with all due respect to the learned theologians, this is nonsense. After a single death, an increase in numbers merely adds a quantitative dimension to the injustice of death. What is unjust is that anyone should die at all. Those who die of AIDS would die anyway eventually. So would those who died in the holocaust. Both are horrific, but in their absence lives would have lasted only a few decades more. The injustice is that any life, even one of ninety-five years, is too short.

Enda offers the Christian response—Jesus died and Jesus rose again. It is an effective response for those of us who believe in Jesus and believe in You—effective

52

sometimes anyway. It will persuade no one who does not want to be persuaded. Ultimately we must make a leap to the conviction that our own life means something or that it does not. If the latter is the case then death is an intolerable injustice. If the former is the case . . . ah, then the matter grows interesting. If the life of a creature that reflects on its own mortality means something, then mortality is somehow transcended.

How?

That, I think, is finally up to You.

July 11

OFF today to lecture at St. Mary of the Woods, thus breaking my long-honored rule against summer lectures. But I figure I owe the Sisters of Providence at least one talk.

To continue on the subject of death. St. Thomas Aquinas is supposed to have had a mystic vision at the end of his life which led him to say of all his philosophical work, "mihi videtur ut pavia,"—"it all seems like dust." Now, in any objective sense of the word, he was wrong. His work is among the greatest intellectual endeavors of human history. It is anything but dust. Doubtless, he knew in some fashion both the value and durability of what he was doing. His judgment has to be seen as comparative. His work was not worthless but compared to what he had seen it had only minute worth.

Fair enough, it seems to me, though I suspect one can make that judgment in all honesty only after the vision. And what judgment can be made by the wife and mother who has loved her children and her husband and made them as happy as she could through their life together? Is her work dust or is it of infinite value, value beyond reckon or measure? Or, to be utterly Catholic about it, are both judgments true? Would not Aquinas, in a less rhetorical mood, admit that his philosophy was a participation in divine knowledge and hence in its own way also of infinite value, even if it were only a small participation?

Thus when I ponder my own life's work, I have to say that it's not much, though some of it will probably perdure. I hope also that some of the good I have tried to do continues to have influence. But compared to who You are and what I believe You have prepared for all who love You, anything that I have done is also dust. But dust is important, is it not? For dust comes from the earth and the earth is our base of life and the foundation of Your creation for us, the source of life and hope. Much of my struggling and effort seems small and unimportant and indeed is small and unimportant. It is also a participation in You which is why I must continue to do it even when I appreciate how small is its objective value. Small, but not utterly worthless because You share in it.

July 17

I HAVE ceased to apologize for missing these reflections when I have house guests because I am now persuaded that the exercise of the virtue of hospitality is a short-range substitute for meditation. I assume You agree or at least understand.

Summer now is officially half over. I am slowing down, though it is neither an instantaneous nor flawless performance, which I also assume You understand.

Please note how much tolerance I'm conceding to You, which tolerance You seem to deserve on the basis of the parables of Jesus, though hardly on the catechesis of the church when I was growing up. In my head I believe the parables. However the catechesis of performance still is strong in my preconscious and unconscious.

There was a neat story in the collection I was reading today. An achieving man outlined all his plans for success. What would happen after he had achieved them all? Well, he would relax and enjoy life. What, asked the wise man, prevents us from enjoying life now?

Oh, boy, do I need to hear that!

July 18

I'VE been watching Bergman movies this week, the result of reading Bob Lauder's book. Characteristically, I chose *"Smiles of a Summer Night"* and *"Summer Interlude"* to watch first because I know from *"Wild Strawberries"* that Bergman has a summer obsession something like mine. Oddly enough, Bob does not note that in his book and I've never seen any reference to it in work on the Bergman films. There is something haunting about the summer "nights" in these three films—in fact they are days that never end. Our Grand Beach summer is not quite like that and not quite like the terribly short winter days with which the Swedes pay for their summer nights.

More to the point, however, Bergman sees summer, and especially summer nights, to be correlated with love and particularly with Young love—on the one hand lovely but brief and on the other a hint of, if not what life means, then of how it should be lived.

To a considerable extent the celibate commitment excludes one from the human love which a summer night primarily refers to. I suppose I miss that, though I was so determined to be a priest that I didn't notice that I missed it when I was the age of Bergman's characters. Sometimes now I wonder if the sacrifice was worth the effort as I watch the church and the clergy do their best to destroy themselves. But that worry is inappropriate in the light of summer and summer love, which are sacraments of Your love, the reason for my commitment.

The Bergman "retrospective" will be an interesting experience precisely because he is an unconscious sacramentalist who rejects the God You are and does not know that You are the Love which he celebrates, the Love which is always vulnerable, since vulnerability is the price of love.

The heroine in last night's film understood that she could not build a wall of invulnerability around herself. Help me to understand the same thing.

July 19

A GRAY, rainy, depressing day here at Grand Beach, made worse by the failure of the electricity for most of the morning. I've been listening to Jack Shea's tapes. He emphasizes the "amazement factor" in religious experience, the amazement which led Jesus to exclaim the Our Father and the amazement over his religious power which led the apostles to beg him to teach them to pray. I am convinced from my own research and storytelling that this is precisely the heart of the religious experience—pure astonishment, pure gratuitous astonishment, or maybe I should say astonishment at the gratuity. That is the essence of religion, no matter how much we may layer other matters on top of the surprise component.

How little astonishment there has been in my life lately. The one surprising incident this summer was the way my creative imagination turned on when I began to write my poem dedicating the picture book to the Daley clan. The images and words raced out of control, absolutely out of control. Astonishment with a vengeance. Not because it was about them, because it was only about them indirectly, but because it was about the City as a sacrament for You. I must listen more to the poetry in me.

It took a couple of weeks to settle down to write the poem, a couple of days to ignite the fire and then a couple of hours to write it.

Astonishment needs quiet and that I don't have enough of. I absolutely need more of it and more poetry too. Please help me to make more room for it in my life.

Last night Bergman's film, *"Dreams of Women,"* was about astonishment and resilency under pressure. Both of the women were treated badly by men, both suffered broken hearts, and both rebounded, much to their own astonishment. Bergman celebrates the astonismenon of life and love.

But one has to make room for it doesn't one?
Again I ask You to help me do so.

July 20

ANOTHER cold, rainy, and busy day as I find that there is work which I must continue to do. Mail and phone, phone and mail. I know that I can't escape them. I know that I shouldn't put this journal and my exercise off to the end of the day. I ought to find time to relax despite the harassment and the responsibilities.

Yet I don't. At this stage today all I can say is help me.

John Shea's tape today is about adoration, the sheer adoring of the power and goodness of God which is what the first petition of the Lord's Prayer is about. Not much of that in my life. How can there be when it is filled with so much business.

Help!

July 21

JACK'S "Our Father" tapes continue to be both disturbing and reassuring. This morning he points out that it is in Your nature to give, that in a certain sense You have no choice but to give. Moreover, to quote the "trailer" in Saint Luke's version of the prayer, "Your father knows what You need." A fortiori does Your mother, since today I am addressing You under Your maternal title (which I find far more appealing, which is not surprising for a man). The "correction" Jack proposes to the prayer of petition as opposed to the human petition is that in the latter we must force the human who possesses something we want to both listen and to be generous, whereas with You, You always listen, always know what we need (which may not be always what we want), and always give with overwhelming love.

The perfect mother!

I believe that completely, even if I don't always live that way. Or even pray to You that way. It's hard to feel affection for such an awsome Mother, though obviously that's what You long for and perhaps even need. Jack quotes Martin Luther as saying that the Christian's prayer is always brief, there is no need to babble like the pagans do to get Your attention. Fair enough, brief and affectionate. I'll try.

Some of the people who survived the Iowa plane crash yesterday said that their survival strengthened their faith in You. They didn't ask the quesiton which one must ask in the face of Jack's vision of You: What about those who didn't survive? They must have prayed too, at the last moment of their lives.

I will not say You didn't hear their prayers. I will only say that You love them, too. You're their affectionate mother, too. Beyond that no one can say anything.

July 24

IN the Shea tapes these days I listen to more about Your prayer. Impressive! The purpose of prayer, even prayers of petition, is to orient the personality so that it will be open to the influence of God's love—the flap feathers on the wings of a bird adjust it to air currents. We may ask for specific things in our prayers but in fact what we are really asking for is You—Your love, the love of the One who hears and responds.

Prayer then is a disposition of interdependence, a reminder to the self that we are creatures who depend on Love and that Love somehow depends also on us.

This dependence angers many contemporary humans. They resent having to depend, they resent that they are creatures, they resent that they are not God.

I'm not sure I would want to be You. Candidly I don't know why You keep the job. Nothing but complaints. And You're certainly not in it for the money!

More seriously I may not explicitly want to be You, but, like everyone else, I'd like to be in complete control of my life. I may not intellectually object to my dependence, but in practice I try to minimize it as best I can. I admit in principle that I'm the creature but try to control as much as possible, try to act like the Creator in whatever way I can. The reason I do that is that I don't possess (enough of) the orientation that Your prayer is designed to inculcate. If one has to be a creature, then one will be the happiest and the most secure if one knows that the Creator loves You and that You can trust Her.

Best of all, I guess, is that the Love continues even when the trust is weak. The openess of personality that the Prayer is designed to produce simply makes one happier and more productive and loving as a creature.

Help me to trust in Your love.

July 25

ONCE again the beginning of this prayer was wiped out by the machine. As I was saying, the experience of You as benign, which is at the heart of the Our Father as well as of the rain prayer of the Aztecs in this morning's reading from Patrick's book, is by no means a monopoly of Jesus. We all have that experience. What is unique about the experience implied by the Our Father is the absolute power of it. Because of His special union with You, Jesus saw more clearly and felt more confidently Your love for him (qualitatively different? Who knows? If it were qualitatively different would Jesus still have been human?). Christianity is nothing more than the expansion of Jesus's consciousness of You, of the Lord's Prayer expanded to the world.

The difficulty is that it is not as strong for us as it was for Jesus. Sure, we know that there is benignity in the cosmos, but it often doesn't seem that such benignity is powerful enough to ward off the powers of darkness at loose in the world. How can You be Love if there is so much sickness, suffering, and death? It's not the intellectual problem of evil that I'm talking about here—that's a reflective problem—it's rather the instinct that the world is a mess and bafflement that benignity could tolerate such a mess.

There's no effective answer to either the problem or the instinct. There is only the persistent experience of benignity, of grace, of love, of Love, of You. The Our Father is a reassertion of the experience of Jesus as we share in it by being his followers, a simple statement of confidence (sometimes quite hesitant) that You will validate Your relationship with us just as You did with Him. We call You our Father because we share You with Jesus, because we share in that most overwhelming experience of Your Grace.

I will try to say the prayer with more attention and confidence. It represents what my faith in You is all about.

Help me to deepen my confidence in my own all too frail and faint experiences of Your goodness.

July 26

ABSOLUTE dependence, total trust—these are the words of such theologians as Schleiermacher and Buber to describe our relationship with You. I won't fight it. It's part of the experience of living, if one pauses for but a moment to reflect on it. We might not like absolute dependence, but the truth of the matter is that we are nonetheless dependent and would be dependent on a much less gracious creator that You seem to be. Odd that Prometheus, who was thought by the ancients to be mad, is a hero for moderns who resent and revolt against being creatures.

Too bad, such revolt, such defiance is not going to work, regardless of how much energy goes into it.

Might a Creator be less generous than You are, a Giver more penurious? That's a good question, I guess, for theologians. Scotus would have had a grand time with it, Sean Dunne the Irishman, to give his proper name. It doesn't argue that You are grace, it rather asks whether grace has to be as generous as we experience it at the penumbra of our lives.

YEAR OF GRACE

My guess is that grace less gracious than You would not have bothered with all the effort of creation.

Is total trust safe, then? I'm not all that good at it, but the issue, it seems to me, is not whether it's safe but whether there's any other choice. We can live defiantly and grow weary of our defiance (like Zorba). We can live fearfully and die a thousand deaths. Or we can live trustfully as the Our Father says we should.

Help me to live in trust, not only in word but in attitude and deed.

July 27

MY head is reeling—Shea's theology (plus others not as good), Bergman films, the slipping away of summer, the reflections in this journal, working on stories, hunting for a new novel theme—I'm on overload tonight. There's so much mystery, so much suffering, so much love. It's all beyond me at the moment.

There was a wedding scene in the film tonight—how happy wedding dances are and how misleading. I can remember maybe the happiest wedding I ever attended, so very very happy. Now . . . . all tragedy. And so many almost as bad. None of the suffering was necessary. No one intervened in these marriages to cause physical tragedy. It was all in their heads, doubtless emotional problems inherited from their families, but not incurable, not preventing creativity and happiness. They made their own beds of tragedy. I tried to prevent them and lost.

I found myself wondering if I made it worse for any of them. Surely I didn't. I guess I didn't help much either, perhaps not as much as a priest might, because I was so concerned about them, because I became a quasi-parent.

It was ten years ago this week that the group blew up on me. I supposed it failed long before that. I'm over the pain now and relieved and have been long since. How I grieve for this sorrow in the lives of so many of them.

Take care of them.

Help me to clear my head a little bit next week.

July 28

MY head is cleared this morning. Nothing like nine hours of sleep to do that.

Back to Shea. The image he sees lurking in the Our Father is of this mighty, benign, gracious power giving Itself of the world, sweeping through the world drawing all together, this is the Father who is in heaven and with us, this is the will which will be done, this is the king which is shaping up.

Well, now!

Since I'm addressing You in Your womanly title today I must note that the Father in heaven is also a Mother in heaven and that the drawing together in unity is, if anything, more a maternal role than a paternal one in the ordinary circumstances.

That Shea and the theologians he relies on are correct in reporting that this was the religious experience of Jesus, I take to be a given. Jesus did experience You in such fashion and used the *abba* metaphor to tell the story of that experience to us—much to the horror of even moderate feminist theologians whom I've been reading (oh my, how ideology destroys the creativity of even the intelligent!). The Our Father is the story that tells us the *abba* metaphor as Jesus experienced it.

Fair enough. Is it our experience too? Is the *abba* experience unique to Jesus or do we also perceive grace (You, that is) the way he did, though perhaps not so profoundly or powerfully or confidently? Or are You, as *abba* (or mama), lurking on the penumbra of my consciousnes with the same scheme for transforming me and everyone else?

Do I understand the story of the Our Father not only from the outside as someone who was taught to pray it but from the inside as someone who can say, "Yeah, I know what He means because I've been there too!"

I guess the answer is clear enough: the "abba/mama" experience is mine too, though not with the transforming power of the parallel experience in Jesus. With me it is dim and distant, the far edges of the penumbra. Nonetheless I know what he's talking about. I indeed have been there, too.

Not only grace, but converging grace, grace drawing all the members of the family together.

Hard task, You've set for Yourself! The kingdom is a long way off, the will is anything but done. How little progress since the time of Jesus. How much resentment and envy and fear and sickness keep us apart. How little we know about keeping our conflicts constructive. How much we are trapped in the paradigms of sin, even when we are aware of the "abba/mama" aura around our lives.

All we can do is try—try to help the king to come, make room for the surging power of Grace. We must listen more carefully to the Voice on the fringe and try to change our relationships so that we are more sensitive to energies You have set lose to draw us together.

July 29

I ALWAYS know when summer is winding down: the raspberry season comes to an end and the Chicago Bears trot off to Plattsville. I don't like those developments, since I'm a summer freak. However, despite all the complaints earlier this has been a good and relaxing summer.

Also I have in my head the first scene of a new novel, about Ireland.

So why complain?

Tonight at Mass I propose to tell a new Mollie Woopie story about the Our Father, using Shea's theme of total dependence on the words "give us this day our daily bread," the point being that daily bread is our life itself.

There are two ways, Jack says, of considering our life: one as a possession which we once did not have and once again will not have but which we now have to protect against all threats; the other is to realize that life is a gift that is given every day, indeed every second. It is pure contingency, pure gratuity, pure grace, not a once for all gift but an ongoing and continuing gift.

Hence we do not cling to it and do not worry about it. Rather we leave the fundamental protection of the gift to the one who gave it and continues to give it, You, that is.

Acknowledging that we receive our daily bread from You is classic creature sense, since our daily bread is actually our daily life. Each morning is a new gift to be treasured and received gratefully. Each evening a time of gratitude for the gift of the day.

Jesus perceived that more powerfully than anyone in history and lived that way. We who are his followers perceive it but dimly and live that way only slightly. I can't claim in my Mollie Woopie story tonight that I live that way. All I can say is that to the extent that we are able to infuse a little of that attitude into our life, the happier we will be.

We are sustained in existence by power that is both loving and determined. The gift will not be taken away even by death—that's what the Lord's prayer means. I must continue to try to say it every morning and every evening as if I really believe in the coming of Your kingdom and the implacability of Your gift.

We are indeed totally dependent, totally contingent, totally gratuitious.

But our dependence is on a mighty lover who also chooses for the success of his scheme to depend on us.

Why did You do that, I wonder? Couldn't You have produced through the evolutionary process a more intelligent and braver partner?

Well, You didn't, so You're stuck with us and we with You.

Give us this day our daily bread.

July 30

I'M tired this rainy Sunday morning, the last Sunday in July. Tired and discouraged. No particular reason save perhaps the strain of entertaining guests and general weariness, even if rain prevented water skiing and forced on me another hour and a half of sleep.

So I'm not going to reflect very much. This is a day one sinks into and let's happen what will happen.

Help me. I love You.

July 31

CRIES AND WHISPERS last night, Bergrman's religious masterpiece in which he asserts, in effect, that there is grace in human love, if not Grace. He advocates, again in effect, gratitude for grace, even if there isn't Grace.

An unarguable position, it seems to me, not only because there is much to be thankful for but also because it is in the nature of our nature to be grateful. One can fault him, obviously, for dodging the question he puts on the lips of the Lutheran pastor in the film: if grace, then why not Grace (as I would rephrase that poor man's agonized cry of the heart)? Or if grace, how come? How account for the love, however tenuous, with which the film ends unless there is Love?

However, those of us who believe in Grace and Love are often not nearly so sensitive to grace and love, which we believe to be the sacraments of the former, as is a man like Bergman who is not so sure. We use our doctrinal beliefs about You, in other words, to ignore or slight the signs of Your presence as they lurk in the world.

My summer session with Bergman is something like

a retreat, a dialogue with an agnostic who is more aware of those events and persons in the world which hint at Your presence than I am.

He is a challenge for my next novel—how sacramental can I make it?

In the meantime help me to be aware of Your presence everywhere as I struggle through this day which begins as gray and cold, and thus fits my emotions on this last day of July, the perfect summer month.

August 2

I TURNED from Bergman to Roehmer last night — *Clare's Knee,* the only one of the early films I have not seen and, according to the critics, one of the best. Like Bergman (and me) he has this summer fixation, though it is a much happier summer, one of amusing little follies instead of great, powerful tragedies. It is also (in this and other films) a glorious, beautiful summer. The lake in this film is almost as lovely as Grand Beach.

If Bergman takes life too seriously Rohmer can be accused of not taking it seriously enough. His people babble endlessly, with serene French confidence that they know what they are talking about when in fact they are merely making themselves look ridiculous. On the other hand there is no malice in his satire.

My vision of summer is different. I view it as more seriously sacramental, more a promise, and more a loss. Last week is appropriate for nostalgia. Yesterday is a treasured memory.

Andrew Greeley

I'm half tempted to write a critical essay about summer, except I think that it would violate the spirit of summer to do so!

How wise of You to provide the seasons (for most of the world anyway) so that we can glory in summer and see You lurking, either through presence or absence, in the wonders of summer.

Help me to get away to the beach today and almost every day for the rest of the summer, even when I have guests, if that be possible.

August 7

THE first Monday in August, cold enough and gray enough to be October. I feel tired and vulnerable, hanging by a thread. I have to fly to San Francisco at the end of the week for the American Sociological Association convention and prepare for guests next week. I don't know why either of the latter should make me feel fragile, except perhaps they represent the slow erosion of the summer.

It is surely true that I hang by a thread even when I don't feel that way. It is also true that this feeling should be an occasion of grace because it reveals reality to me. But there is an unhealthy touch of depression about the way I feel today. Maybe it's only physical weariness—guests and perhaps too much exercise. Maybe it's the pressure of the obligations and responsibilities which pile up on my desk each day—too much mail, too many phone calls to make and to answer. Maybe it's a sense of another summer being wasted—rest and relaxation but not enough of either.

Moreover I slept nine hours last night, so I have no grounds for feeling tired like I do. I guess it's a sense of being harassed rather than physical exhaustion, of being overwhelmed by obligations that I'd rather not have.

Or am I only describing the human condition?

I should like to spend this day relaxing since it is too cool to do anything else. I won't be able to do so, but at least I should try with Your help to be more relaxed as the day goes on, more bright and cheerful on the phone if nothing else.

And to be that way in gratitude to You and not because of yet another obligation.

August 8

SUCH a creature of light and darkness I am. As soon as the clouds cleared away yesterday I felt fine again and proceded to organize the rest of the summer, adding dinners and guests that I would not have thought about adding in the dark morning. I've known for a long time that I'm one of those beings who are especially sensitive to light, but, oddly, I have paid little attention to that aspect of my organism. On dark days I should moderate my fatigue and on bright days my enthusiasm. Except that, since You made me the way I am, there is also grace in these swings of mood, properly understood. The light is a grace for action and planning the dark for rest and relaxation.

71

Yesterday was very funny in one respect: I was so weary during the dark morning that I contemplated not swimming at all. This was, I told myself, a day for rest. Then when the sun came out I swam a mile, twice the distance I have been swimming all summer—with no discernible ill effects this morning. It is an incident to keep in mind as I search for the signs of grace working in my organism.

I'm now in the fifth month of this journal and wish to thank You for inspiring me to try it. It's been a most useful technique of prayer and reflection, with more impact on my life than any other prayer form I've ever tried. Help me to continue to keep it.

Having said that, I must also add, now with the sense that You understand and don't mind, that I'll be away from the computer screen for three days while flying to San Francisco for the sociology meetings.

Where they had an earthquake this morning!

August 13

BACK from SF, exhausted (two mild tremors from the San Andreas Fault) and with guests. No time.

August 17

It's been a terrible week.

How can I really say that? I have attended the ASA meetings and entertained guests, both good things to do. In the process, however, I have stayed away from this journal which has become something of a haven of peace and meaning in my life and rushed around at a frantic pace. I have consoled myself with the truth that You love me even if for short or long periods I'm caught up in this maelstrom.

Yet I look at the summer slipping away, note that I have another week of travel and guests and grow discouraged. I am surely more relaxed than I was at the beginning of the summer, but not really relaxed yet—not many days this month of August have seen me on the beach or even the deck. Yesterday was the only day "off" during the week and I never really got out of the house after water skiing in the morning.

I don't what to do, if there is anything at all to do. Autumn will not be heavy and yet people call to invade it, take time away from me, demand that I do things for them, things which are pointless from every angle except that they have or think they have some reason for making demands on me.

I am tired already and I am in the middle of what is supposed to be a vacation.

Help me.

August 18

THE guests are gone and I now begin ten days of relative peace. I like to have guests. I like even to take care of them. Yet it becomes a heavy routine after a while. I don't want to give it up—just as I don't want to give up most of the other things I do in life. Yet the demands that I make on myself and others make on me become enormous. Strange, is it not, that in my youth I thought that virtue was doing as much as possible. Now I think virtue is doing less than I do so that there is more time to pray and relax, reflect and contemplate, create and revise.

I haven't been to the beach in a long time. Tomorrow I will start again and try to return to a more meditative mode—something that ought to be easy in the midst of the surpassing beauty which You have provided for this tag-end-of-summer day.

August 19

IN my scripture reading today I encountered that superb story Your Son told about the prodigal son and the indulgent father. There is no doubt that the story reveals the intimate experience of Jesus with God—You that is. When push comes to shove that story is the key challege to faith. It is not merely a nice story about a father who is a bit of a pushover for his wandering son, it is a story about what You're like. If one accepts the notion that You love the way the Father did, then there is nothing about which to worry. Everything will indeed be all right. Only it is so hard, in the face of evidence that You don't care about us, to believe that Jesus had an accurate fix on what You're like.

Mind You I'm not denying that Jesus was right. In my head I believe that he was. The problem is translating that intellectual acceptance into a dominating principle of everyday life, especially when there seems so much to worry about—the next book, the church, the government, the various enemies who hate, failing health, old age, etc.

In fact these are not arguments against Your love, but about the imperfections of human life which You did not promise to eliminate—any more than You promised to protect Jesus from death. The promise is merely that Your love will vindicate itself in the end—as it did with Jesus.

Having played the propositional game about the story of the Prodigal Son, I must also now assert that Jesus' stories, like all stories, do not really admit of such analysis, not after a certain point. They are stories which illumine and offer possibilities for living. While we must, I guess, analzye them, we ought not to analzye them to death. Rather we ought to say, that's the way Jesus experienced God. If one permits oneself even the beginning of such an experience, one can also begin to live as Jesus did, not immune from the limitations of the human condition, but happy and brave in the face of them.

Help me, please Lady Wisdom, to bask in the glow of that story and to live, at least a little bit, in its illumination.

August 21

I'VE been listening to tapes about narrative theology in the car these days and I'm surprised by how much of the magic and wonder of story have gone out of my life.

Andrew Greeley

If the salt is useless when it loses its savor, what happens to the storyteller when he loses his sense of wonder, his awareness of the magic of creation?

Belden Lane, the theologian on the tapes, observes how much we have become "head" persons (and left brain at that) to the exclusion of all else in our selfhood and Your creation. It is certainly true that for all the imagery at work in my stories I personally am mostly a head person, prosaic, cognitive. I am a person of wonder and surprise and magic and hope when I sit at this machine to write my stories, but that wonder and surprise and magic slip away when I get up from here to answer the phone, open the mail, deal with the problems of ordinary life.

August 22

ONLY a few more skiing days left. I confess that I'm almost glad. It's fun, but every day it kind of wears You out. However, the issue of why I am not more open to wonder or to be even more explicit, glory, is deeper than merely physical exhaustion from water skiing and swimming every day.

As I try to reflect on that weird aspect of my life I must admit that I have more reason for surprise than most priests of my generation. Indeed I ought to be endlessly surprised, astonished each time a new novel appears and that anyone, much less hundreds of thousands of people, buys it.

Surely for that excitement, that astonishment, I am grateful to You—and to tell the truth I fear that I have never appreciated it enough to respond with much gratitude. The success of my novels is an event, like other events, but not a source of surprise or wonder or joy.

Maybe I do too much or too many other things besides the novels. Maybe I should step back from the sociology and the journalism and concentrate more on story telling. Quit sociology when I was ahead after the lead article in the current ASR. Except there is something less than responsive to wonder in that reaction too.

I guess I always come back to the same point, not enough time to pray and reflect—and to rejoice.

There is another aspect of it too. I know that You understand, though lots of folk wouldn't should they read these lines. While I am often accused of taking myself too seriously, it is probably more the truth to say that I don't take my work seriously enough. In many respects that's a good thing because if I did the battering in the priesthood might drive me even more to the fringes. But in fact, I view a new novel like a Sunday homily—something that I had to do to meet a responsibility and then it is done and that's that. Thus *Saint Valentine's Night* appears next week and there is no joy in the book or treasuring of it.

But it is in fact a splendid story with a powerful illumination about human love. Despite the usual anger it will stir up in many folks, it will cause wonder in more and give them a hint of Your glory. How can I not rejoice about being part of such a phenomenon?

Help me, Dearest One, to rejoice and to wonder about what You've helped me to do.

August 23

HELP me to keep my joy serene over *Saint Valentine's Night.*

August 24

YOU will have noted, Dear One, that I have begun to address You affectionately, as I would a woman lover. How long a time has been required before I take the metaphor seriously. Despite John of the Cross, and my own research on the utility of a womanly image of You for men, and despite the metaphors in my fiction, only now do I somehow feel at ease with the language of tenderness in my conversations with You.

I have created images of You, my Love, in the character who interjects Herself in my autobiography, images which of course are only metaphors for You, but which are nonetheless attractive and accurate as far as they go, but I have not spoken to You in language which the images seem to demand. Why so reticient? Perhaps I am afraid to use the language of love for fear I will be caught in it? Perhaps I am embarrassed by emotion, even though it is unlikely that anyone besides me will read these pages. Perhaps I do not want to appear to be a fool.

And now, I'm sure, only because You have become fed up with my prayers of intellect instead of intimacy. Somehow I have hesitated—by not even reflecting on the possibility that the language of tender intimacy that one would use in bed with a lover is the most appropriate language for prayer. You have brought those hesitations to an end, fond and beautiful lover, and I find that, as my language changes, feelings of joy and surrender burst out of me. I'm sure I will stumble and hesitate, as do all shy and inexperienced neophyte lovers, but with Your help I will never turn away.

I also understand that, like all passionate lovers, You want to hear my passionate response, in fact need to hear it. Such an idea violates theology but it does not violate the scriptures, especially the prophets. Moreover, not surprisingly, the language of love creates the emotions of love and they in turn transform life.

August 25

HOW far can this metaphor be pushed? It is of the nature of human loves that they be vulnerable, that one must be delicate and tender in relating to them, that one must protect them from being hurt. Surely I must so treat those whom I love the most, particularly those of the other sex. There is nothing more demanding or more exhilirating than delicacy and gentleness with a woman one loves.

Does this apply to You, My Love, who extend far beyond the lovely blue planet Neptune, which is on TV this morning? (I hope You don't mind my picturing You as Neptune blue—and marveling that the color has been there all along although we now see it for the first time; it is, incidentally, the same color that we used to call "Blessed Mother Blue.") Must Your vulnerability be protected as I would protect the vulnerability of a beloved woman? Do You wish to be cradled in my love as I do in Yours?

What a startling thought! At first, I think that perhaps such a notion pushes the metaphor too far. You are the Lady of the Universe, the cause and end of all. Why would You need my protection? Perhaps it is not in the nature of love to need the other's tender delicacy, the others sensitive concern? Surely the infinite Love is not vulnerable, are You?

And yet . . . and yet . . . do You not permit Yourself to be pictured as vulnerable in the Bible, especially in the prophets and most especially in the Incarnation? So apparently there is aspect of You, my Beloved, that correlates however remotely with what we humans think of as a sensitivity and vulnerability, that needs to be treated with delicacy and protected tenderly.

More than that. It would appear that the metaphor, to the extent that it fails, fails because of defect. If You are indeed vulernable, then Your vulnerability must be infinite, You must absorb all the pain in the universe, You must need all the protection You can get, all the delicacy that Your creation has to offer. Since each relationship is of infinite importance, You must need delicacy from each one You love and infinitely at that.

Not only must I picture myself as resting peacefully in Your arms, I must picture my own arms around You, reassuring, nurturing, caring. You are a Love who needs my affection, my passionate response to Your fragility.

All of that boggles the mind. But it is nonetheless true, even more true than I can imagine. You need my protection more than the most appealingly vulnerable woman I have ever known.

That will take some time to absorb.

August 27

THE last Sunday of summer, for all practical purposes. Labor Day is next week but the kids start school tomorrow, so Grand Beach will be as empty as a tomb. I hate this bittersweet time. I'll be fine, my love, after Labor Day when September starts and I begin serious work on my next novel. Autumn in Chicago is a good time. But the end of summer is miserable. One more summer gone. Not many left. But thank You for the joys of this one.

As usual I did not relax as much as I wanted to. Every day, every week, every month—they all go by too quickly. Yet my pace did slow down, if only marginally. I hope during the days of September to work on the book in the morning and spend time on the beach in the afternoon, weather permitting. And I'm off tomorrow morning for New York and Washington for the new book. Maybe it won't be such a madcap autumn as last year. Not much chance though.

To return to my discovery of You as vulnerable lover.

The language of this journal is perhaps not as stiff as the language of my book *Complaints Against God* and not nearly as passionate as the prayer meditations in *The Cardinal Virtues,* almost as though I am afraid to put on my own lips the passion for You that my protagonist feels.

Yet, if I reflect on how I would behave towards an appealing, wounded woman who needs my support and help, I perhaps begin to understand how I should relate to You. I would be (and am, as far as that goes) thoughtful, sensitive, patient, considerate. I call, I think of things to cheer such a one up, I worry about her, I reassure her.

It is that a proper posture vis-a-vis You, my Dearest One? If love means anything and if as I said in my last entry the prophets and the Incarnation mean anything, it surely is. Love can do no other.

To put it cognitively, as I still am, (and in the language of theology) it would be wrong not to take the metaphor to that point in trying to know You. There is an apsect of You which corresponds to that part of the metaphor, only more so. You are in a certain sense even more vulnerable, and hence more demanding of my sensitivity, than any human woman might be.

It is scary to think that one has that power over God. My Greek philosophical and theological training rebels against such a conclusion to reflecting on the metaphor. But, is not the essence of revelation, the essence of the incarnation, the confirmation of such a conclusion?

I can talk about this reflectively. I cannot yet live it or even feel it very deeply, because it seems so strange. I'll keep trying.

August 28

I'M up at six for the trip to New York and feeling tired. As usual, my dearest love, I dread the venture, even though it's only two nights away from here. You did not design me to travel. Keep me safe and reasonably relaxed during the trip. Please.

The other side of the metaphor of love about which I wrote yesterday is that I am dependent on You, dear one. Every love is a sharing of vulnerabilities. I do my best in my ordinary relationships to protect myself against vulnerability (in which respect I am like everyone else of the species). Especially in my relationships with women, do I play the role of the protector who does not need protection, of the strong one who does not need the strength of anyone else. I would have made a fine husband perhaps for a weak and passive woman but not for a vigorous and aggressive woman—although the latter are those I find most attractive.

I am, it is to be feared, afraid to let go of my own security, to risk myself with others. I may trust people too readily (as we have ample evidence) but the trust is superficial, with my work perhaps but not with myself.

So maybe the reason that I was—and continue to be afraid—of intimacy with You is that I fear intimacy with anyone.

Not good, not good at all. Help me to respond to the challenge of intimacy that You offer.

More than that on this weary Monday morning at the end of summer I cannot say.

August 31

I'M back from the trip to New York and Washington and thoroughly wiped out. I do not improve as a traveler with age. Now it's the last day of August—already—and summer seems to have slipped through my fingers without my having anything to show for it.

That's air travel fatigue showing and, as You well know, I ought not to be taken seriously at a time when I'm caught in that fatigue. I console myself with a thought that at least a wife and family don't have to endure me in this condition. On the other hand You do have to put up with me and if the metaphor on which I'm reflecting these days means anything, it means that when I'm discouraged and tired and grumpy that affects You too.

So I should try to contain my weariness for Your sake?

What else could the metaphor mean?

And what can I say but that I will try?

September 3

A GLORIOUS Labor Day weekend so far, skiing both days and probability of more skiing tomorrow. Summer ends with a bang.

About the end of summer I must meditate more in the days to come, not that I haven't meditated about that often in the past, but perhaps in the context of my new sense of the love between the two of us I may understand it better. Or at least be at ease with the story of summer's end.

From the point of view of eternity, it makes no difference. Indeed from the point of view of time, it makes precious little difference.

Your love for me is not diminished, nor is the contribution of my books to the lives of people.

LABOR DAY

LABOR DAY, the technical end of summer and the beginning of the new year. I hate it, even if I'm going to hang around here pretty much to the end of the month, with excursions into the city for masses and anniversaries and weddings and baptisms and Bears games.

This is my twenty-fourth Labor Day at Grand Beach, a lot more have gone by than I'm likely to have in the future, but the problem today is that it has finally dawned on me that as much as I enjoy this place and as much as it renews me (however partially), I have never given You, my love, much gratitude for it. It's been a great grace in my life and I am most fortunate to be able to have it. I am deeply and profoundly grateful for the opportunity, the friendships, the peace, the conversations, the work, the sky, the waves, the Lake—everything about it.

In my crowded life I have not reveled in this haven nearly as much as I ought to. For that I'm sorry. Help me to enjoy it more in the days and weeks and, should You be willing, years ahead.

I pray for all of those whom I loved so much that they may find peace and happiness in their lives. But I am eternally grateful for this splendid place which has brought me so much peace and happiness. Even now when I think about how wonderful it is, my end-of-summer discouragement fades away.

But despite problems out of the past, this place has been mostly benign in my life. I realize that I should have thanked You more and I'm sorry I did not. I also realize that full enjoyment of its beauty and its peace is the best kind of thanks I can offer. So in the next four weeks, while I'm here working on my new novel, I shall endeavor to give myself over as best I can to its peace and and joy.

September 6

ONE conclusion follows inevitably from the love metaphor, not so much a theological or logical conclusion as an immediate intuition. Lovers take care of one another. Therefore You are taking care of me and I, wildly enough, have a responsibility for taking care of You. You cannot, for reasons that we humans cannot fully understand, protect us from all evil, but You will care for us, me, in the end. Therefore it is safe to trust in You. You will validate us as You validate Jesus. Here is the core of my faith and of my love.

Hence the end of summer is a tragedy, though, as human tragedies go, a minor one, save that it indicates the passage of time and the nearness of death. However, it is only temporary because eternal summer waits in the arms of Love. In Your arms.

Hence I am sad about returning to Chicago for the rest of the week on this gloomy, humid day. But my sadness ought to be modified by the truth that ultimate reality is summer and not the end of summer. If You are love, to switch the metaphors, You are also summer and summer perdures over that which destroys it.

Or so I believe, not merely intellectually (and intellectually the doubts swing back and forth) but intuitively with the knowledge of love. I must reflect more and more that I am in the grip of a powerful and passionate love which will never let me go.

And that I also have that Love in my arms, the most mysterious of all Christian mystical insights and the one I'm trying to celebrate in the present novel.

To which I turn now, dedicating my work to celebrating You.

September 9

MY LOVE,

I wonder if I have ever properly thanked You for those days. Christ the King parish was one of the critical formative experiences of my life. But have I ever really said thank You for it.

So let me do so now. They were great years, tense, frustrating, embarrassing, maddening, but still wonderful. I am what I am in great part because of those ten years and I still celebrate them in my stories. I am grateful for the ten years themselves, for all I learned, for the grace which came from the people, for the friends I made, for the memories that are still with me, for the rejuvenation which yesterday's visit created for me.

Can I go back? Leo said at the lake the other day that You can never go back. I wonder. I'd sure like to try. It would be fun. I'm sure I would not be disappointed. I don't expect things to be the way they used to be, but they still would be fascinating.

And I'm grateful that during the day I remembered You and thanked You for the opportunity of renewal.

Help me to continue to remember You, love You, and thank You each day.

September 10

A SEPTEMBER Sunday in Chicago—cloudly, rainy, and a Bears game. No doubt about it, autumn is upon us. It was good to get back to weekend Mass at St. Mary of the Woods. Saying Mass, presiding over the Eucharist, is a more rewarding experience each time I do it. For that great grace and for the grace of SMW, not Christ the King, but still wonderful, I am deeply grateful. Help me to continue to say Mass in such a way as to suggest some of the joy of Your love for us, a joy I feel at Mass now more than at any other time in my life.

September 11

THE clouds cleared away and yesterday was glorious, for which much thanks. And the Chicago teams won so there is much rejoicing in the city. And I slept well last night which means that the previous nights' poor sleep was the result of the transition and not of some creeping depression.

How much a creature of time and place I am. Even an hour change in time zone and a shift of less than a hundred miles from one locale to another, from one set of routine habits to another, upsets me. I guess I am a local not only in my theory and conviction but also in my physiology.

Since I am in a modality these days of giving You thanks for those graces I've taken for granted through the years I now want to thank You for the gifts of the places I live, not only efficient environments in which I can work but also beautiful environments where Your goodness is reflected. For those much thanks indeed. Help me to continue to thank You during the course of the day and to be aware of Your loving presence and Your presence needed to be loved wherever I am and whatever I am doing, especially this week when I must do the transcontinental jet thing to Los Angeles and Boston and home.

September 12

I'M off on the transcontinental jaunt today, Los Angeles for the Home program and then Boston for the immigration meeting at Woods Hole. I console myself with the thought that it's only three plane flights and Woods Hole would have been two to begin with, so it's not really all that bad.

Except You and I know that it is bad and that it will take the whole weekend to get over it. Such exhaustion goes with the territory, I guess. I must think of You often and give myself over in loving trust to You and relax as best I can.

My sleep was disturbed again last night, but this time by the new novel. I wrote thirty pages yesterday, an exercise which is guaranteed to keep me restless at night. The characters and the plot obsess me when I'm involved in a story and I'm surely involved now.

In the litany of gratitude which I have been reciting these days, I want to thank You for the novels. I still can't quite believe that I write books that millions of people read. My ability to spin yarns is an enormous gift to which I have no right and of whose existence I was unaware a dozen years ago. It infuriates a lot of people who resent the fact that I have the gift and they don't. I can't help that, I guess. I realize that the gift is a gift and that it is meant to be used in Your service. I'm not perfect in that regard (or in anything else) but I do think the stories succeed as parables and the mail I get confirms that, regardless of what some of the envious think and say. The gift is sometimes a burden, as it is just now while I'm being swept along by the story. However it is mostly fun and exciting and adds a dimension to my life that did not exist twelve years ago, a second (or third or fourth maybe) career that has helped to keep me young in heart, among the other things it has accomplished.

So I thank You for it with all my heart and pledge to keep on using it in Your service.

September 16

I'M back from the three-day transcontinental trip, as usual exhausted, depressed, and with battered sinuses. There's nothing like such a venture to write "finis" to the summer. Now as this last weekend of calendar summer begins—and it looks like it will be a fine weekend—I am as worn out as if there wasn't a summer to begin with. However, I imagine I'll bounce back more quickly, especially since I'm leaving for Grand Beach tomorrow for two final weeks and more work on my new novel, a story which continued to haunt my dreams while I was wandering across the country.

I hope at Grand Beach not only to write in the morning but to use most of the rest of the day, free from the distractions of high summer, to reflect and pray. Please help me to do so.

You were on my mind and in my heart during the journey, though only barely and not as much as a human love would have been. In my own defense for this negligence, I was not designed to fly in airplanes, as You well know, having designed me.

But while it is approriate for me to express my sorrow that I didn't think of You more, it would not be appropriate to think that You stop loving me. That love is implacable and definitive and nothing takes it away.

Help me to be conscious of that love and to respond to it through this glorious weekend.

September 17

I'M always taken aback when people say after Mass that it was a very entertaining Mass or a very enjoyable Mass. I'm tempted to say that the Mass isn't entertainment but worship. Then I realize that it is in fact a joyous celebration and that it should be enjoyable and entertaining. To the extent that the ceremonies of Mass are dull and ponderous and dragged out and precious they fail to live up to the central symbolism of joyous thanksgiving.

Some of the most joyous moments in my life are now at Mass, not merely in theological theory but in actual experience. This joy results from a gradual shift in my own attitude towards the ceremony, a shift caused by both new theory and practical experience. If one makes the Mass fun for kids, then everyone learns about Your love from it. There isn't much scared awe left after such an experience, but there's a lot of love and laughter which, on the record it seems to me, You prefer to awe. There is a risk of course that the celebrant who celebrates this way will lose a sense of the sacred altogether for himself and the congregation. I am conscious of this danger and want to go right up to the line and stop short. So far, so good, I think, but I must continue to be careful to balance the sacred and the casual in the right amounts. It never hurts the congregation to see a celebrant who is happy when he presides over the Eucharist.

The challenge for me, and the purpose of this reflection, is to translate that happy celebrant at Mass into a happy celebrant in all phases of my life. The Mass then becomes, in a curious re-creation of the theology of my seminary days the focus of my life.

Why? Because of the dialogue of joy between priest and people. As I argue in *The Cardinal Virtues,* the spirituality of the priest for the most part comes up from the people—which is why I give thanks to You this Sunday in September for the people at St. Mary of the Woods who are, however temporarily, my people.

September 18

IN my reading this morning there seems heavy emphasis on detachment, on not caring, on being disengaged from the concerns and problems of this world. This emphasis represents the eastern mystical and spiritual tradition and it is based on the wisdom that one can not serve two masters, or given the metaphor which is directing my present reflections, two lovers, two mistresses.

I can hardly deny the importance of such wisdom. Yet I cannot reject the western wisdom of social concern and involvement, however much this might be distorted and perverted by those who think that social involvement ("relevance"), often of a Marxist variety, is a substitute or a virtual substitute for prayer and reflection. Somehow the two must be balanced, intimacy with You and dedication to Your world and Your people. Westerner that I am, my propensity is always in the direction of concern, involvement, commitment and away from reflection and prayer. However, I have always wanted more detachment, more perspective, more prayer. These notes have been a great help in that direction.

It is not so much a question of giving up my activities, though perhaps some of them must be given up in a process of letting go (I don't have to do everything, do I?), as of listening and watching, praying and reflecting, relaxing and laughing—like I am at Mass.

Teach us to care and not to care, Eliot said. I make that prayer mine, especially for these two weeks. Grant that the phone and the mail and the novel I'm working on do not interfere with this quasi-retreat experience, an experience which can make or break, in a certain sense, this summer.

Teach me to care and not to care.

September 19

WHO CARES?

Such is the punch line in one of the Buddhist stories that I read this morning. Most of the things I worry about and care about are not, even in the short run and from the this-world viewpoint, worth caring about.

You love me and will always love me and take care of me. In that love I cannot allow my peace or my happiness or my serenity to be disturbed by those events which are not worth caring about and those false friends who cannot accept what You made me.

I write those words and I mean them, but I do not mean them completely or perfectly. I do not need, however, to be perfect because You, my wonderful one, will make up for my imperfections in the power of Your love.

Help me to realize more deeply and more powerfully in the course of this day how powerful that love is and how few things are worth really caring about.

September 20

IT'S 5:30 A.M. and I'm up on my novel-writing schedule, in part because I don't want to miss a nice afternoon on the beach (such as I had yesterday and for which much thanks) but also because the story prevents me from a peaceful night's sleep despite yesterday's swim and long walk.

Do You find our stories as fascinating as I find the stories of my characters? I used the storyteller metaphor for You in *God Game*—You love us the way a storyteller loves his creatures. So I have to conclude that You are as obsessed with the stories we write together with You of our lives as I am with my Dermot and Nualla in their search for truth and treasure and love.

Except, and here's where human metaphors always err by defect rather than excess. You are more obsessed with us than I am with my characters. Our propensity is always to think that metaphors for You—vulnerability to those who love You and fascination with Your creatures —go too far, exaggerate, skirt the edge of heresy. In fact just the opposite is the case—they don't go far enough. You are more vulnerable than the most vulnerable of human lovers, more obsessed with us than any storyteller is with his characters, more in passionate love with us, to use the central metaphor, than any human lover could possibly be.

I believe these truths completely, though they are so staggering that I have yet to absorb them into all of my personality—and probably never will as long as I live. At any rate help me plunge into their depths so that I can revel in them more, especially today when the obsession with Dermot and Nualla as they travel west in search of their grail will surely haunt me all day long.

September 21

LADY LOVE,

I'm so tired this morning at 5:20, despite a peaceful night's sleep relatively untroubled by the characters in my story. Even with my schedule of working only in the morning and early evening on the story and taking the afternoon off to enjoy the fine weather and to relax, I'm still being worn by the story—and by the interruptions.

I am patient with the people who call and stop by and I should be patient. They have no way of knowing what an obsession the story becomes when it is in full flight as it is now. There is relative peace from now to nine o'clock but even then I must go into New Buffalo about my car for the third time this week, an interruption in this early morning period of peace that I don't need.

I'm not complaining. I'm grateful for the ability to tell stories, for the fun of writing one, and for the zest of this particular story. I'm just explaining why I'm tired and trusting in Your love to accept me even when I'm tired.

I thought of You often yesterday. Help me to do so today too and to be less compulsive, should that be possible as I continue to work on this story about Your love.

September 23

THE first day of autumn or rather the first full day with autumn arriving last night at 8:40—and a huge equinox storm with fifty-five mile an hour winds sweeping across the lake and the temperature falling 20 degrees. Summer is over both officially and practically.

I like autumn. It's a busy, lovely, exhilarating season in Chicago. And it's now time to go back to Chicago. The Grand Beach part of the year is over and I am actually eager to finish this story and return to the city where I belong for the next several months. I thank You for the excitement of autumn and for having a city to return to.

Autumn also reminds me that I am in the autumn, perhaps even the winter of my life. That is a melancholy thought but one which I must also face with clear and realistic eyes. I don't have all that many summers left. I'm grateful for all of them and I trust Your love to sustain me through what lies ahead.

September 24

I AM grateful that I am still alive.

The auto accident yesterday was not, I think, my fault. But it might have been. I'm convinced that I had the green light and the other driver ran the red. I looked back immediately after and his light was red.

Yet I'm not sure because I knew what a tense state I was in. No one was hurt and my car was barely damaged. Thank You for that, too.

It was all so quick and I was so shook, my mouth drained so dry that I couldn't talk.

I feel responsible even though the more I reflect on it the more certain I am that I had a green light. I was so tense from all the things I have to do this weekend and from working on the novel and from the transition between Grand Beach and Chicago where I'm writing this morning before returning for the final week at Grand Beach and working on the story.

And now I'll have three more mornings of going to New Buffalo and interrupting the work.

When I'm doing a story I should really cut myself off

from the world and not move. The complexities of life mixed with writing not only deprive me of peace, they make my life dangerous.

I'm still shook. I'll be extra careful driving back this afternoon.

Thank You for the warning, please take care of me. Please.

September 25

4:25 ON MONDAY MORNING.

I don't like getting up at this hour but it's the only way I can work on my book and not be interrupted. I go to bed at eight after turning off the phone and that gives me four hours to work in the morning before the world begins to intrude. Except last night the alarm went off in the middle of the night and the cops broke into my house to make sure that no one else had broken in.

It's clear to me writing this novel that there is no way I can work on one and relax the rest of the day, unless the rest of the world is cut off, which is to say, no phones, no mail and no driving back and forth to anywhere—and especially not a weekend like the last two days, in which I spend nine hours in the car. I should arrange my life that way the next time I try to write something—and I could do that even in Chicago if necessary, but only by doing what is difficult, that is protecting the month completely beforehand.

I'm sorry that I've let myself get into such a state. I have failed to realize—after twenty-two novels!—that creation of a story is a demanding and compelling work for which I should create the best possible atmosphere for myself and not try to do everything else I always do.

Next time around I'll try to realize.

Keeping his journal of dialogue with You is a big help in forcing me to think constructively about my life and the reasons I am so overwhelmed.

There is such a difference at these times between what I believe and how I am that I am ashamed of myself. I know You still love me and take care of me, strengthen my faith and my resolve.

September 28

THE novel is finished and the revisions are done so that the first draft may be considered complete. I like it, but then I always like them first time around. Thank You for the grace of being a storyteller and for the grace of this story about two very gifted and very shy children.

Tomorrow I return to Chicago for the autumn, always a lovely time in the city—for that too I'm grateful.

The novel exhausted me, as they usually do. I wish those who complain about my output knew how hard the work is. It wouldn't matter, I suppose, if they did.

My resolution to spend some of this last two-week period up here relaxing was a total failure. I did usually stop working at noon on the story, but there were, of course, other things to occupy my time, despite the beautiful weather.

I suppose fasting and writing a novel at the same time is not an advisable combination. Yet September seems to be the month to do both.

I thank You for the weather and the walks each day on the beach and for the beach to walk on. Grant that this transition back to the city may be easier than the others or that it will disbturb me less.

Help me to keep my cool during autumn.

I love You.

October 3

I AM having a hard time adjusting to a routine here, part of the usual transition crisis, I guess. It was somehow easier to do these reflections when I was at Grand Beach pounding away at the novel every day and walking on the beach in the afternoon. Under those circumstances my awareness of the presence of Your love was much clearer than it is in the hectic, catch-up life of early October.

Also my spiritual reading seems to have become more routine and less challenging.

Help me to reorient my life so that there is more sanity and order in it, at least internal order, at least an awareness that I am working out of a context of Your love. I also seem to have lost touch with my summer insight about You as a vulnerable lover although my novel was based on that theme. Help me to recover that poignant and powerful image today and in the days ahead, particularly as the hazy, bittersweet blanket of Indian summer wraps itself around me.

I want to live my life as a sacrament of Your love, yet I am so distracted and so tired at the end of the day.

October 5

I READ a novel yesterday about Jesus—for a review in the *Washington Post*. It was well researched and and well written. Like so many other recent fictional works on Jesus it tried to explain away the mystery, to make Jesus acceptable to the "modern mind"—which means the mind of fallen away liberal Protestants like the author and his friends. The book is sincere and well intentioned and somehow solipistic: the author would be the first one in history to get back beyond the New Testament to the "real" Jesus, that is, the liberal Protestant Jesus.

It doesn't work of course because the essence of Jesus is mystery. Eliminate the mystery and You lose Jesus. Sign him up for Your cause and, whoever has joined Your staff, it turns out not to be Jesus.

I reflect on this book just now because I am tired again and still disoriented almost a week after my return to Chicago, hardly in any physical or psychological situation to note mystery, even though signs of wonder and surprise are all around me (like *Rosenkavilier* which I saw last night). Help me, especially through the coming weekend, to get my act together and to be aware of Your presence and love through the day.

I know You love me just as much in these "down" times as You do in other times.

Andrew Greeley

October 6

I'VE started to read the New Testament, beginning at the beginning with Saint Matthew's Gospel, which we know how wasn't written by Matthew and wasn't the first Gospel either, not that either of those points matters much. It's hard to read the stories with the wonder and the surprise they deserve because I have heard them so often. Yet as I was going through Matthew's account of the Infancy narratives this morning I couldn't help thinking about Leslie Whidden's attempt to explain them away in the novel about Demas I reviewed for the *Washington Post*. The issue is not whether they are literally true (I personally suspect that there is more literal truth in them than some of the scripture types are willing to admit, but that is not really the point, is it?) but whether they convey the wonder and the surprise which the early Christians found in their encounter with Jesus. I suppose if I were being precise about it from my own perspective I'd say that their encounter with Jesus awakened them to the wonder and surprise which was already in the world and of which they had been unaware—the Jesus event deepened human perceptions about the mystery that they had already dimly perceived.

There is so much wonder and mystery in my own life. You have surrounded me with it, inundated me with it, drenched me in it, swept me away with it.

On this October morning I have so many reasons to rejoice in the mystery in my life. I thank You for all of them. Help me to enjoy them and to realize that they are but faint hints of the wonders and surprises that are yet to come. Don't let me get so tired, so weary, so over-worked that my sensitivity to surprise is erased. Help me to be as open to wonder as Joseph and Mary were when the astonishing happened to them.

October 8

THE serenity slipped away this morning. I'm not sure why.

Maybe it was the complaint to the pastor after Mass yesterday that he would have to get rid of me because I was more a "showman" than a priest. Leo was not intimidated, though like all pastors he worries about complaints. He knows that there are scores of people who like the way I say Mass.

Such complainers trouble me because of their narrow, rigid, and punitive approach to religion. I suppose we made them that way or helped their parents to make them that way.

This particular complaint troubled me a little more, no, a lot more, because I have been wondering whether my informal, joyous, demonstrative approach to the liturgy might not be going too far—not wondering enough to change the way I say Mass, I might add, but enough to trouble me a bit.

I have no doubt that most people like the kids around the altar, the forceful reading and recitation of the prayers, the stories, the games with little kids. But is this designed to make them like me or to like the Mass? Is it possible to separate these things? If You celebrate the liturgy as if it is a celebration people will like You. If You are nice to their kids they will like You. Jesus was nice to kids, too.

I don't know. Eucharist means thanksgiving. If we think of the Thanksgiving festival in November, we realize that it is an exuberant, celebratory, familial feast—that is the best way to thank God.

I don't want to contaminate such celebrations with self-promotion. On the other hand I don't want to abandon it (and I won't) because of a few complaints, even complaints that poke at my own self-doubts. Maybe this complaint will help me to be not more cautious in the way I celebrate the Eucharist but more aware of the possibility of self-deception in my celebrations.

I also must remind myself that totally disinterested and dispassionate behavior is impossible in the human condition and not necessary for You to sustain Your love for me. You love me regardless. If I am trying to do the liturgy the way it ought to be done, then You love me however much there might be admixtures of other motivations creeping into my behavior.

I guess the drumbeat of criticism is getting to me again, the harsh rigid judgmental attitude that the church has inculcated for centuries—the opposite of Jesus. I must reflect more on that in the days ahead. The criticism gets to me I guess especially because some of my own personality is still shaped by it.

October 9

COLUMBUS DAY, celebrated by some and not by others and on the wrong day. Somehow this nation ought to get its holidays lined up right.

The passage from Saint Matt today says that the power of God is at hand and in the psalm David asks that You be a rock and fortress against his enemies.

David knew he had enemies. Today he might be called a paranoid for suspecting that he had enemies. God knows (You *do*) that I have enemies. Just now I really need a rock and a fortress against them. I need Your power as it is sweeping through the world to fend them off. I realize that Your power does not necessarily mean that the enemies will be routed, only that they cannot take away my happiness or my union with You. I was depressed all day yesterday and woke up early this morning, a sure sign of depression.

The content of the depression is the same as always— why bother? Why work so hard and be rewarded with animosity?

I know the answer to that question of course. I work because of love, I work for the same reason Jesus did even though he knew he'd encounter the reaction of emnity that ultimately killed him.

All I'm saying or trying to say today is that it's getting to me and I'm weary. I won't quit. You know that. I won't give in to depression. You know that, too. But right now it's very hard and I need help and encouragement and love.

Help me. Help me to help myself. Thy kingdom come.

Andrew Greeley

October 10

STILL depressed. I'll keep trying to ward off the feelings but they'll have to run their course, I guess.

"Come follow me," the Lord says in today's reading from the Gospel, "and I will make You fishers of men."

Thirty-five years ago I responded to that invitation, thinking it meant being a priest. It turns out that it is one of the meanings, though we have no monopoly on it and that many of us don't do much fishing—rather we pollute the lake.

It seemed so simple then, be a priest and be a fisher of men. Now it's all so complicated.

In my role as a marginal scholar and storyteller I must spend so much of my time fighting off those who are supposed to be my allies—and who would call this assertion which You and I know to be perfectly true, paranoia.

All of this, I suppose, is a reflection on the imperfection of the human condition. No goals, even the ones most sincerely sought and most innocently pursued, can ever be achieved without trouble and conflict, without the kinds of struggles which seem to contaminate the purity of the pursuit.

That sounds more Protestant than Catholic, doesn't it? But I said contaminated, not perverted. My desire to be a priest as a young lad may have been tainted by the conflicts of life, it may slip temporarily away from my immediate vision, but it is still there and still good, still unperverted by the thirty-five years of wearying conflict with which I have struggled since ordination.

Help me to sustain that vision, particularly in times of discouragement.

October 11

TODAY Matthew depicts Jesus as going around Palestine preaching the good news that the power of God is nigh. Very good news indeed, now as well as then, and good news that I must keep in mind in these days of October discouragement. Moreover the Irish poem I read this morning by Derek Mahon about a kid waiting to be born and his hunger for life is also pertinent. For I believe, do I not, that the child's hunger for life, my own hunger for life, are in fact invitations to which I am asked to respond, that life is an invitation to a love affair in which I am the invitee.

Or, more precisely, I believe that the invitee to a love affair metaphor fails by defect—it is not a strong enough metaphor: the reality of the meaning of life is more dazzling, more glorious, more demanding, more exciting than the metaphor reveals.

That's what Jesus went around preaching; it is as good as it was then and as news as it was then. It's also as too good to be true now as it was then.

Help me to believe it and live it.

Also, by way of a note, one of the problems this week is that I don't have an immediate project. The novel is finished and there are no sociology data available yet. I guess I am not very good these days at sitting back and waiting patiently. I have to learn once again from GKC the advantages of doing nothing.

October 17

SIX days since the last entry. What can I say? I went off to Grand Beach without a computer, planning on three days of rest. Instead I continued to be depressed, couldn't sleep very well and came down with a migrane headache. It's all over now, for which much thanks, but I am exhausted and only beginning to bounce back.

The transition may be over by now and my head is above water. Now it's time to go back to trying to be the light of the world as every lover of Yours must try to be.

Help me to recapture my tranquility and to think of You and Your love often during this and subsequent days.

October 18

I'M still bogged down in work, depression, and gloom. It seems that I'm always rushing from one thing to another with no time to think or plan or to relax. Even those moments of recreation, such as watching Woody Allen's *Crimes and Misdemeanors* last night, become an obligation to be discharged instead of an interlude of enlightenment to be enjoyed.

Some of this may be physiological, though at least last night I was able to sleep well, despite the stimulation of the film and the continued controversy about me and my life which just now is at fever pitch. Maybe I will readjust in the next couple of days to life in Chicago, sleep regularly again and feel the burden of depression lifting.

I hope so.

Our first reaction when leaving the film was that it was a portrait of a moral universe without love, or Love. On reflection, however, we concluded that of the three options offered by Woody, the one represented by the blind rabbi dancing with his daughter represents the possibility of a universe animated by love, a possibility which the director finds most attractive but of whose reality he is not yet convinced.

The point for me is that I am convinced of that reality yet so much of my life is lived in the ambiences of the other characters—Woody and Martin Landau.

I believe in a moral universe and I believe in Your love, Your vulnerable love indeed. I have not the slightest doubt about that reality. I am grateful that I was born into a tradition which has taught me about You and for the grace to continue to embrace that tradition.

I will not be too hard on myself and say that I don't live like I believe in Your love. I do. It does make a difference, but not nearly enough difference, my life is not yet permeated and animated by that conviction.

I must continue to try. Help me.

October 19

Whatever it was that possessed me for the last couple of weeks is gone, just as quickly and as abruptly as it came. I'm sleeping well again and the depression is gone.

Must have been more physical than anything else. I've had interludes like this before, but since I wasn't keeping this journal of prayers I wasn't quite as much aware of them till they were over.

An example of how thick the gloom is of those interludes is that yesterday I did not reflect on the earthquake in San Francisco. I was too groggy, too dense, too oppressed even to be aware of the tragedy.

Thank You, first of all that my friends are all unhurt, particularly Mike and his family, about whom I was worried and whom I called yesterday morning.

What am I to make of such catastrophes? Why do some commuters on the Nimitz Freeway die and others on the Bay Bridge survive? Why are some people's homes destroyed and others remain undamaged? Why do some live by the slightest chance and others die also by the slightest chance?

There are, I understand, no answers to those questions. Yet I am disturbed when some survivors say on TV that You saved them and do not even think it strange that You apparently did not save others.

I'd like to be able to accept such a version: You are responsible for the near miss survivors but not for the near hit casualties. I ask myself whether that would not be a rather strange sort of God, however—one who takes credit for the successes and shrugs off the failures, one who does her best to protect all her children and sometimes succeeds and sometimes fails.

The bottom line is that You do love all Your children and take care of them one way or another—even those poor commuters on the freeway. That I believe. As for the rest of it, I could ponder and agonize over it all week and still be no nearer a solution than I am now. You suffered, I know, with those who died and mourn with those who mourn. You are injured whenever one of Your children is injured. You would protect them if You could. Why You can't and why You don't are questions completely beyond me. But I do believe in You as a vulnerable lover who hurts when any one of us is hurt and that has to be where we begin. You didn't want the earthquake. Why You couldn't or wouldn't stop it is unanswerable. But You didn't want it and You sorrow with all the suffering.

Help me to sorrow with You, to grieve with those who grieve, to ache with those who ache—not obsessively but in the corner of my person that is reserved for grief.

Thank You again for jolting me out of whatever strange lethargy it was which possessed me for the last couple of weeks. Protect me from its return.

And thank You too for the lesson in human love which hints at what You are like as a vulnerable lover.

October 20

HOW come on October 20 there are four inches of snow on this city?

It's not fair!

Of course, if I'm true to the theology I reflected on yesterday, I would have to conclude that if we suffer (slightly) over the coming of winter a month too early, so You suffer with us.

You don't think it's fair either, is that true?

That question, written about a very minor problem,

points right at the center of the problem of the vulnerability of God over against the power of God. I believe in both and I have no idea and never will how the two are combined, save that in the end the power of the vulnerable God is triumphant.

You will mix both qualities in the final analysis, in the end, whatever that temporal clause means. Until then it is the vulnerability which should hold my attention.

So I should stop worrying about it, as best I can, and concentrate on Your vulnerability which is a fact of revelation and the one that is immediately pertinent for my spiritual life.

I have pondered this truth before and have shied away from it because it is so overwhelming: You are to be imagined as a fragile woman who has been hurt and I should treat You with the delicacy and tenderness with which I would relate to such a woman—and, if she should be someone I love—delicacy and tenderness mixed with passion.

That is a big order, even with a human lover. With someone like You it is quite overwhelming—to be passionately gentle and tender and delicate and affectionate with a wounded God!

Is that what You want? Is that what, to be even bolder, You need from me?

How can I deny it?

Yet how do I live it?

In my head I know it's true. The task is to adjust my life, prayer and ordinary, so that I live with the care that is required in such a relationship.

This weekend at the lake, amid the hoopla of the Notre Dame/Southern Cal game (You'll be in real trouble with a lot of my neighbors if You lose), I will try to work this out poetically because the images will be more powerful for me and more effective in poetry than I can make them in prose.

I end today's reflection and prayer with a sense of unease. I don't want the task of being responsible for You as I would be for a human metaphor. It's too big a task. Why should You need my tenderness and care? You're God aren't You?

But You need tender care and want it, that's certain. So I must try to provide it as best I can.

You'll have to settle for something considerably less than perfection, which I suppose I hardly need tell You.

October 21

THE wind continues to blow off Lake Michigan. Six inches of snow already and it's still October.

Big Joke!

I'm off to watch N.D. play Southern Cal today. The faith is on the line. I presume that You're neutral.

More seriously, I am writing this in the early morning before I try my hand at poetry to articulate more effectively the metaphor of You as a vulnerable God. Maybe tomorow I'll have some poems to enter into this journal of prayers.

Now I want to turn to the subject of prayer. Why should one pray to You if You are not capable in the short run of protecting us from harm? Why, for example, pray that we be protected from earthquakes if Your short-term power can't make earthquakes go away? All our instincts are to pray to some higher power for protection—and like the characters in Verdi operas blame You when something goes wrong. We pray because we need to depend on some higher power. You want us to pray because, in the metaphor within which I am working, You are a vulnerable God who wants our love. But what effect does this have on the outcomes? I mean, if one has a vulnerable lover one is nice to that lover and protects that lover. If prayer does that, and I presume it does, then I'm not opposed to prayer.

But does it affect outcomes? When I pray for those whom I love who have cancer, do my prayers make any difference in their survival. The prayers may reassure me and them and perhaps even You (if the metaphor is proper that's a legitimate insight). But beyond those surely desirable outcomes does it make any further difference?

It might be replied (You might reply, my patient friend) that in the long run Your power and Your vulnerability are the same thing and that You will take care of the cancer victims and the earthquake victims and those who pray for them and that therefore our prayers will be heard. Fair enough, but You'll take care of them anyway so what difference do the prayers make?

This is not to say that I will stop praying because, as I have said, prayer is necessary for those who pray. My problem is what impact my prayers have on a suffering God, on You my suffering love?

As a tentative answer I would suggest that somehow, in this less than perfect world over which You seem to have less than perfect short-run control, our prayers become resources for You. Maybe Mike Hout was right yesterday when he said, "thanks be to God" that the earthquake was during the evening rush hour instead of the morning rush hour. Maybe in the present order of things (for mysterious reasons I cannot understand) our prayers do not enable You to prevent an earthquake (You seem to be bound by plate techtonics for the moment) but prevent them from being as disastrous as they might be. Our prayers in this view of things enhance Your power to prevent short-term tragedies from being worse than they are.

That is the kind of tentative answer which would surely please no unbeliever and maybe not very many believers either. But for the moment it is the best I can do as I try to understand a little better the mystery of Your power and Your vulnerable love.

October 22

THE PATHOS OF GOD (After Rabbi Abraham Joshua Heschel)

Like a geranium wilting in a drought
Or like a weeping child lost in crowded store
A lovely woman, alone, frightened, hurt,
My sensitive and tender care implores.
I wipe away her tears and beg a smile;
I want to heal, to cherish, to ease her pain,
To gently say that in a little while
She'll laugh and love and begin her life again.
Is her pathos a sacrament of God
Who, some say, weeps each time a baby cries?

Andrew Greeley

Is the desire she stirs in me the barest hint
Of Her ultimate, astonishing surprise?
Can it be—O truly dazzling wonderment —
That God requires my most delicate abandonment?

October 23

SATURDAY night I had a nightmare experience, wide awake.

I'd spent much of the day at the Notre Dame game festivities, a pleasant if exhausting and probably excessive exercise. I fell asleep immediately and then woke about one o'clock with memories of all the mistakes, blunders, failures, errors in judgment, and stupidities I had committed during my life as a priest. They rolled before the eyes of my memory with extraordinary vividness, as though they had all happened that afternoon instead of over thirty-five-and-a-half years. The conclusion—obvious it seemed at the moment—was that I had wasted my priesthood.

Anyway, in the morning the world looked much better. Everything in my life is not a mistake or a failure. Moreover, You do not expect perfection from anyone, only effort. For a lot of the mistakes I have long since apologized one way or another. Still I'll have a busy purgatory—which I think will be interesting and even fun since reconciliations and apologies are fun.

Nonetheless, it was a hellish interlude, in the strict sense of the word, because I felt, in that state half way between sleep and wakefulness, that I was cut off from all possibility of reconciliation and expiation and therefore cut off from You.

Obviously, that's not true. But there must be somewhere in the depths of my soul that fear—a fear based not so much on reality as on an exaggerated notion of the perfection I demand of myself. You forgive my mistakes, that I know. There is a part of me that doesn't want to forgive them, which repressess them and holds them ready to be used as charges against me.

Ugh!

October 24

OUR third Indian summer continues, for which many, many thanks. My reflections during the last several days would indicate that You can claim credit for nice events and disclaim responsibility for the unpleasant ones, which is nice work if You can get it. I don't understand these matters so I will thank You for the good things that happen and commiserate with You because You suffer as we do for the bad things.

Which is the way mothers act, especially if they are Irish.

The reading in Matthew today is about serving two masters, You and profane concerns—which is I think the proper way to interpret the passage because there are a lot of other profane concerns besides money and many of them even more demanding.

One can have two lovers, two mistresses, two women if one is a man only with the consequence of being torn

in opposite directions. Many of the classic tragedies and
not a few of the classic comedies are written around that
theme. In everyday life, however, the love of You and
concern about the world are not simple alternatives.

Even if one loves You, one must give some care to life
here, especially because life here is the way to You, the
way to serve You, the way to demonstrate one's love.

My own problem is less money than my work. How
do I harmonize my commitment to my work and love
for You, especially since the commitment is based on
love, although, when it gets out of hand, it interferes with
love.

Yesterday I was swept up in an orgy of work which
I need to get done before I leave for Ireland next week.
And need to do in the midst of a week which is busy
with other and trivial but necessary exercises.

I suppose the operative word here is "need." I don't
absolutely have to clear the desk before I go, but it would
be nice if I could.

However, such closure is not worth losing my serenity over, not worth exhaustion at the end of the day, not
worth ill-temper every time I am interrupted on the
phone.

Yet how do I get perspective when I'm caught up in
a project which I like and which is, in some sense, important? All I can say on that subject is that my life-time
record is not all that impressive.

Today will be another busy, crazy, over-crowded day.
Help me to keep You in mind during the course of it and
that I am serving You and not merely the projects I want
to finish.

October 25

AS YOU know, one of my good friends is having surgery today. Please grant that she may be all right. Which now I take to mean that my prayers are a resource that You use to do Your best, under the limitations I don't understand to make her well.

The reading from the Sermon on the Mount is about not worrying. Ha!

The same morning I read this I also read in the *Times* about Nelson Algren and how he squandered the money he made on his novels. It was a nice counterpoint. I haven't spent my money on eating and drinking and such like, but perhaps I have given it away recklessly, so that now I must be concerned a little about how well my books do, a problem I never had before. Nice irony indeed.

I don't regret the generosity. I do regret that it wasn't a little more balanced. I have a hard time saying no to requests, which is a lot better than having a hard time saying yes, isn't it?

In any event it is all absurd. At worst I will be better off than 99% of the people in the country and if I have to curtail my generosity that is too bad but it can't be helped, can it? I hate to let others down, but perhaps they have depended on me too much. A budget won't hurt.

None of this is worth worrying about as an immediate problem, though it might be one by the spring. And even then it is not worth worrying about in the sense of letting it become an obsession, which is what Jesus is talking about in the gospel.

You do love me and You will take care of me—in the long run which, as Lord Keynes said, is the time when we're all dead. But that's all right; it's the long run that counts if one has any faith.

So in the shorter run, as Jesus shrewdly puts it, anxious thought does not add one cubit to my height (as Bill Cosby would have said, what's a cubit?) and I must not let myself get depressed over the problems, most of which don't exist in the real world anyway.

October 27

I'VE finished reading in the Sermon on the Mount this morning. The difficulty with it as a compendium of densely packed proverbs is that from long habit one reads it as a unit and does not pause to reflect on each of the sayings the way one normally would with such a collection. I think this time around I've gone more slowly and listened more carefully. Even then, however, the sayings must be read in conjunction with the parables which are much more dynamic and which constitute, I believe, the religious matrix in which the sayings must be understood.

The end of the Sermon is more parable than saying, the story of the two homes, one built on solid rock and the other on shifting sands, a parable appropriate both for the end of the collection of sayings and for this time with the memory of the earthquake fresh in our minds.

I wonder this morning as I struggle to discharge all the work that needs to be done before I leave for Ireland how solid is the rock on which I have constructed my house. It has survived so far and there have been some storms and quakes, though, God knows (You do) that the storms and quakes thus far have been rather minor. Might it be, however, that the marginal, variegated life I live is in itself a dune of shifting sands?

I don't think that is true, but it is not merely a rhetorical question. I worry sometimes about the kind of life I live with its multiple projects and its rapid movement. I believe that it is the sort of life to which You have called me—certainly I didn't choose it myself. If I had my druthers, I would be very much a local. Yet there are spiritual and physical dangers involved in such a life that I perhaps have not always taken seriously enough.

My geographic, occupational, intellectual, and personal bases are constantly shifting. My spiritual and religious base must therefore be rock solid, even more solid than those of others who are not shifting so much in other respects. I need more prayer, more reflection, and less frantic movement.

That seems to be a theme which runs through all these reflections. I don't seem to have improved much. Still I'm trying and I need Your help more than ever.

October 29

SUNDAY evening, the Indian summer continues, perfectly splendid. And the Bears won. For all this goodness, thanks.

I have pretty much cleared away the work which needs

to be done before I go to Ireland so that this week may be relatively peaceful and I may leave for Ireland a little less frantic than I have on past trips.

I'll have to see whether this unaccustomed prudence and foresight really lasts. Help me to stick to it because November will be a tough month.

My scripture today is Matthew's account of the healing of the leper (skin disease the new translation calls it more accurately), only one and not the added material about ten and only one returning for thanks.

In this verison the emphasis is on the healing ministry of Jesus, a major theme of the scriptures which has been abused by some of the miracle working crazies. The healing of Jesus is primarily spiritual and religious, an easing of emotional and psychological pain which may also have a physical impact.

I must not let my distaste for the lunatic fringe interfere with my realization that a priest ought to be in the healing business. Jesus' healing reveals Your healing concern for those You love. Help me to be a source of healing for others, someone who can ease their pain.

I've been pretty good at this sometimes and terrible other times, the latter mostly because I have permitted myself to be distracted from it by the pile of projects with which I surround myself.

Help me to heal.

October 30

MORE about the healing of Jesus in today's reading. It's a theme which correlates with my shy children theme and the pathos of God theme. Mostly we are in life to heal others. Erica Jong remarks somewhere that we should wait till we are forty to marry because then we know that the purpose of love is to take care of someone else and be cared for by someone else—a theme utterly at odds with the narcissism of the day, the concentration on internal feelings and processes. You can't heal someone else when You are obsessed with Yourself.

However narcissism, as someone remarked, begins at home. There's plenty of it on the loose in our society and it is not limited to those under forty who are products of the Woodstock culture.

I know that to the extent I am preoccupied by myself, worried about myself, closed in on my own problems and fears, I am not able to concentrate on the pain of others. One can not be obsessed with self and heal others at the same time.

Obviously there is a balance to be sought. We must take legitimate care of ourselves. If we don't, we have found another, an opposite pathology. The theme of some of the novels of Greene and Bernanos, that one could will one's damnation out of concern for others, is wrong (and sick). A healthy regard for self is essential to heal others.

It is obsession with self and not healthy regard that interferes with healing. As You know my self-obsession is intermittent (I hasten to add in defense, though You don't need to hear a defense, that in this respect I am not unique but part of the human condition). One of the burdens of being God is that You can't escape from others in self-obsession. You have to heal all the time. I can't do that or be expected to do that unless and until I become God, which is not part of the game plan.

Andrew Greeley

Yet I can heal more and not merely in those times when the conditioned reflexes of the priesthood are activated or when love unleashes its own habits. Help me to be more aware of the pain of others—as You are—and to ease whatever pain I can, however I can.

October 31

THIS has been a truly crazy day. I had almost nothing scheduled except lunch. Nonetheless the time filled up quickly. It's now 4:30 and I have not been to the pool or opened this journal until now. Not a very good preparation for the trip to Ireland. And Thursday and Saturday morning have filled up too.

This has to stop, somehow, some way.

A point I have not reflected on enough about Jesus as healer is that I am the object of such healing as well as the subject of healing for others. Jesus came to heal me of my pain and suffering. It is foolish and perhaps a little arrogant for me to think that I am not included, as I have in the last few days when I've reflected on my role as a healer. I one of the healees too, and God knows at this crazy moment with a phone conversation going on while I type this and listen to the Bears news on TV.

Part of my problem today is the stubborn conviction that I want to see a movie tonight to celebrate Halloween which means I must get through a lot of the craziness that intervenes.

Yeah, I need healing all right.

November 1

I SAW *Shocker* last night and it was great fun, an absolutely perfect Halloween film with both the good and bad dead coming back and the good triumphing decisively —even more decisively than the horror genre requires hope to conquer dream. This festival is an attempt by the Church to Christianize the old Celtic feast of Sahmain (as a "witch" informed us in the *New York Times* yesterday), one that perhaps at last has been successful since the trick-or-treaters are likely to be younger and more adorable and utterly harmless.

Yet the festival perhaps was not totally wrong in its original form. It was based on the belief that at transition times (like now, the beginning of winter, the way the Celts reckoned it) the boundaries between the living and the dead were thin and people could cross back and forth between them.

Halloween (now mostly in fun) and the horror genre rest on that insight—despite the skepticism of modern science it is still possible to be in contact with and haunted by the dead. If You will, a pop culture version of the Communion of Saints.

If one believes in life after death (and most people do) then it is not unreasonable to think that they are close to us at least some of the time. One need not believe in ghosts or hauntings to accept that fact. Moreover, my own research (as well as Erlandur's) shows that most contacts with the dead are benign rather than scary (most like Allison and not like Horace in last night's film).

Well, at a more general level, Halloween stands for surprise and wonder and indirectly for You as a God of surprise and wonder—like all lovers stand for surprise and wonder. Halloween intervenes in our mundane world with a promise of surprise.

I needed some surprise last night and the hope, I might almost say the religious hope, in the film was a pleasant surprise.

I think maybe I'll have to see that Woody Allen film again to search once more for the surprise in it.

Help me always to be open to the wonder You have strewn all about.

November 2

MORE on Halloween.

In late afternoon of the day, I encountered, in the lobby of the building, a little girl (about two, I should think) dressed as a pumpkin—and attracting quite a bit of attention for herself, attention that she didn't mind, although she was clearly tired from her trick-or-treat labors.

I announced to the crowd that she wasn't really a little girl dressed like a punpkin, but a pumpkin dressed like a little girl.

She considered this possibility thoughtfully and then grinned. She was too a little girl, she insisted. Nonetheless, the thought that she might be a pumpkin disguised as a little girl was clearly intriguing. Wouldn't that surprise her mommy and daddy?

These three days, I conclude, are days of surprise and wonder—days when the kids get a chance to add to the wonder which is already in their lives and when adults (save for Scrooge types) get a chance to enjoy their kids' wonder and become children for a few moments again themselves.

You can't beat it.

The loss of our capacity to wonder is one of the most terrible prices of growing up, an unnecessary price, and one that poets and storytellers and saints refuse to pay.

Science and some kinds of theology contribute to the decline of wonder by insisting that there is no room for surprise in a scientifically understood universe—as if the universe itself isn't a surprise! And as if quantum physics doesn't multiply surprise!

You're the ultimate trick-or-treater. Characteristically, You want both tricks and treats from us and offer more of the same in response.

I believe that. I believe that the universe is filled with wonder. I believe that all the surprises in life are a reflection of Your love. I believe that Halloween is one more trick You use to surprise us and to make us wonder about You.

Alas, as I hardly need tell You, I don't always live that way. I'm moving into a very difficult month now, filled with travel and activity. Help my sense of wonder, my openness to surprise to flourish despite this hustle and hassle.

November 4

I'M leaving for Dublin tonight and bringing my laptop with hopes of sustaining at least some of this journal while I'm away. Last time around I didn't do very well. I probably won't this time either but I'll try.

I'm reasonably relaxed, considering that I've been running for the last forty-eight hours, trying to get ready. I hope I don't fall apart like I usually do on a trip. I'm going to try to get a lot of sunlight in Dublin the first two days to see if that cure works. I realize that it's not my fault that I freak out when I travel and that You love me just as much when I am wiped out by jet travel. Still it would be nice to be reasonably conscious while I'm in Ireland.

And to think of You often and to remember Your love and to see all the signs of Your presence that exist everywhere but especially in the sogged isle of my ancestors.

Take care of me on the trip and bring me home safe and well and happy.

Dublin, November 5

IT WAS a cold clear afternoon when I arrived and I walked in the sunlight for two hours. We'll see if light does indeed set my internal clock to zero after two days and eliminate the effects of jet lag.

Travel is hard work and I'm exhausted, but not destroyed altogether, as the folks here would say.

I thank You for the safe trip and my friends in Dublin and for the comfortable place at which I stayed. If traveling is hard for me now, what would it have been a hundred or even thirty years ago?

I'm too tired to say much more than that I love You and I will be back tomorrow.

Please continue to take care of me.

November 6, Dublin

I SLEPT well last night, thank You very much, and am wide awake on this sunny morning in Dublin and raring to go. In a way I regret that I did not become fascinated by this town much earlier in life. There is a lot of interesting and tragic history here—a good thing for me that my grandparents got out of Ireland when they did.

A day and a half ago I was in Chicago, now I'm in Dublin's fair city. No big deal, don't we do things like that all the time?

Yet physiologically we're still upright, bi-pedal apes, with the same internal processes that we had when we began to roam around the savannahs of Africa—and precious little more physical strength than we had a couple of million years ago. But we've been clever enough to build for ourselves ingenious little tools—like the 747—which can transport us in very little time to any place on the planet to which we want to go, quite without any regard for our biological limitations. We're even clever enough to begin to devise ways to accelerate the catching up of our biological clocks.

I'll know in a day or two whether this direct light system works as advertised.

Do I wonder?

Well, maybe. But the point I'm trying to make over my early morning tea is that we are very clever little apes at most things and not very bright at all when it comes to living at peace with one another or enjoying the evidence of Your love which is all around us or at coming to terms with our own mortality.

There's the irony, isn't it, dear one? Our reflective consciousness is the key to all our cleverness and also the cause of our tragic sense of our own mortality and all the flaws (all seven of the cardinal sins) which flow from the fact of that mortality.

Physiologically I ought not to be here at all. But I and my fellows are clever enough to overcome those barriers. Can we overcome the barriers to amity among ourselves and love of You?

Well, it won't be done today, will it now?

I'm already sounding like a real Irishman!

Take care of me today. Help me to think of You often.

Dublin, November 7

A gray, drizzly day. Typical of Dublin weather. Most of my jet lag seems to be over, courtesy of the direct light. However, the depression which accompanies foreign travel now has taken possession of my soul (aided by the fact that I left the immersion coil for my tea on last night and started a minor fire). It doesn't take much in the way of change or weariness to penetrate to that level of my soul where I am depressed, perhaps all the time.

Or maybe only discouraged.

I keep getting the feeling that I've worked terribly hard and have little to show for my work, except animosity and rejection.

So stated, my Dear One, such a feeling is absurd. Obviously hundreds of thousands, perhaps millions of people have benefitted at least somewhat from my work. I do have a mail box parish, as Mark Harris said in his article. There are no rational grounds for my discouragement or depression or whatever it is. The hatred and the envy, particularly of other priests, is a minor aggravation in comparison.

So the discouragement is weariness talking. Or maybe only mortality. Or, more likely the two of them combined.

And the sun in the sky, which is what is supposed to happen this afternoon, will probably change most of it.

So I can only offer You myself this morning with my usual jet travel discouragement and ask for Your help and Your patience and Your continued love.

And, just now when I'm feeling so fragile, Your protection.

Dublin, November 8

OFF this early morning to Cork and back this evening. It's pouring rain which is what happens in Dublin, I guess. Take care of me today. Help me to remember You often and on this melancholy pilgrimage to the site of Michael Collins' death to reflect on my own mortality and how ephemeral are all life's problems and accomplishments.

Everything but faith and love.

Dublin, November 9

THE pilgrimage to Michael Collins' shrine yesterday was a melancholy one despite the lovely weather and the beautiful West Cork scenery. He ought not to have died so young. The history of Ireland and of Europe would have been very different if he had survived. Worse still, no one intended to kill him. This country has had a rough, rough history.

Yet the human condition is a rough, rough story. None of us ought to die. There is too much art and ingenuity gone into the making of the human person to tolerate its short lifespan. Why, one might ask You, do You produce such a complex, interesting, and ingenious creature, only to let it wither and die after a few score years?

Why would not this creature be permitted to live as long as, let us say, a redwood tree. Think of how much it could accomplish with that lifespan.

Or how much bad!

And no matter how long the life span, it would still not want to die. It would still be flawed by its fear of death and by all the weaknesses that its consciousness of its own mortality produces.

I think, as I often do when I reflect on this subject, that You could have arranged matters more wisely.

I am, my sweet love, only too ready to admit that You know what You're doing and that this is Your creation (as You told Job) and not mine. Moreover I accept Your wisdom on the matter, not that in the final analysis I have any choice.

I know You love all Your creatures great and small and You especially love this odd human creature which can do so much good and so much harm and that You have prepared for it great suprises and wonders yet to come.

And I know You love me. I know there are surprises in store for me which make this Dublin weather seem mild by comparison.

Nonetheless I want to go on record as saying that I am grateful for the Dublin weather which just now is better than Chicago's.

Dublin, November 10

I'LL be glad to go home—as I always am as a trip wears on. Even though this has been better than any so far in my life because the sunlight does indeed beat the jet lag, I am tied to a place and a routine.

I had a fit of discouragement yesterday, but it went away, for which much thanks.

New ideas for the novel continue to whirl in my head, which is one of the reasons for the trip.

But everything I was supposed to accomplish has been accomplished. It is time to go home.

Take care of me and protect me, help me to be aware always of Your love and of Your need for my love.

Help me to respect and admire these people who are so like me and yet so different from me.

Dublin, November 11

ONLY one more day in Dublin. The week has swept by rapidly. All my assigned work done, good coversation enjoyed, too much food eaten and none of the drink taken. It is the best trip abroad that I've ever had and yet it will be good, so good, to get back home.

I've been reading Maeve Binchy's latest book. As is often the case there is a compassionate portrait of a priest. It made me think about my own time in the priesthood. The man in the story is totally different from me, a curate moving from place to place with little thought of anything but taking care of the people who come to him. No big dreams or big plans, no involvement in the world beyond his current parish.

After ordination I was a man of enormous energy and big dreams. The parish context was not enough for me, especially because, in the particular parish in which I worked, the restraints on even ordinary parochial work (talking to people after Mass on Sunday) were so circumscribed by the pastor.

Yet I never wanted to leave that parish and have always wanted to return. The desire to be free of the old feudal restraints was, I think, more powerful than the desire to gain national attention, a thought which never would have occured to me. I had things to say about the condition of the Church which I wanted to say and which I wanted others to hear. What happened as a result was a surprise.

Moreover one must follow one's own instinct, listen to the sounds of one's own drummer, be responsive to the promptings of the Spirit speaking to one's own spirit. Not to do so would be the worst of infidelities. I need not be ashamed of what I have become nor admit that my motivations, mixed as are all human motivations, were basically selfish and ambitious.

However, there is still an important point that I must always remember. Perhaps it is easier not to be self-seeking in the role of the priest in Maeve's story (note, my love, I say perhaps—a lot of "simple" priests are self-seeking, too). Surely in the crazy life I live on the margins of the Church and the priesthood, I must be more sensitive than some others (who are not on the fringes) to the danger of too much self-preoccupation—especially since necessary self-defense pushes one in that direction anyway.

It will become a serious problem only when I decide that it is no problem at all.

Help me to be aware of the risks and always conscious of my dependence on You and Your love.

Dublin, November 12

IN a half-hour, my love, I leave for the airport and out of here to New York. It shows how much a home person I am that, although I feel fine and this was a great trip, I wish I were going to Chicago instead. To get back to my work? Well partly, but mostly to get home.

If heaven is a home will I be equally happy to go there? I hope so. I do believe that while this life is a home and one to be treasured, there is another home elsewhere that will truly be home. I believe that my raw faith, which I share with everyone, in the purposefulness of life, is indeed implicitly a faith in such a home where You will wait for me with maternal, spousal love. I believe that at the center of the message of Your son Jesus is a confirmation of a love which is stronger than death, a love which we know obscurely without Jesus and with much more clarity once we know him.

I believe that death is a homecoming, as I have so often said in my funeral sermons. At least I believe it most of the time and all the time when push comes to shove.

Nonetheless, death is scary and I am in no hurry to find out, if only because it's a home to which I've never been and about which I know almost nothing except that You have prepared it for those who love You.

Anyway, thanks for the pleasant and fruitful trip. Take me home to Chicago safely and help me to bounce back from the trip as quickly as possible.

New York, November 13

THE Irish birthrate is going down towards the European average, but You wouldn't notice it in Dublin—or any of the other places I was last week. Moreover the kids seem to be in charge. They are treated affectionately and respectfully and they seem to respond by acting responsibly most of the time.

The Irish have always liked kids and they still do. And why not? Kids represent the future, the power of life over death, the best of our hopes even when the present looks pretty grim. Perhaps Americans don't like kids so much anymore because the present is so good and the future seems so dubious.

Kids affect me in a curious fashion. On the one hand, I'm a kid freak. I like them and they like me—possibly because they see someone much like themselves. On the other hand they make me feel sad because I realize how much disappointment, frustration, and suffering lies ahead of them. The serene joy with which the little kid skips down the street will not last (the joy of my nieces and nephews as small ones did not last into adulthood). Life is not as blithe an experience as they think it will be.

Perhaps we don't do such a good job of raising them. We force them to grow up too quickly, to cope with the difficulties of life before they have learned to appreciate its joys.

I'm not sure about any of these things, especially since this morning I'm exhausted from the trip. Yet when I see movies of myself as a kid I see there a joy in that little boy that I have never known since. How did I lose it? Was it inevitable? Can I recapture some of that joy?

I hope so. More on that tomorrow when I'm less wiped out.

November 15

IT'S 5:50 Chicago time and I'm in the air just out of La Guardia and thoroughly beat from the trip.

The light cure for jet lag seems to work—which makes me not a good traveler, for that You did not design me, but a passable traveler.

I'm tired and I'm heading back to a mountain of work. Two sets of galleys to read, a manuscript to finish, and a novel to revise after the Irish trip. None of these have to be done before nightfall or even before I leave for Seattle on Monday. But the days are crowded and I'll be rushed even if I don't rush myself.

And I must do my Christmas shopping.

After a lifetime of rushing at this part of the year I am not likely to much better this year. But I'll try. And I'll need Your help. Keeping this journal has had a great payoff on my spiritual life. I don't know why I didn't think of it before—or why You didn't plant the idea in my head.

It helped me to think of You more often during the trip, except at the end when my exhaustion in New York turned me into a zombie. So maybe I can ease into this holiday season with a little less chaos and confusion. I hope so.

The Today Show tape of Chicago neighborhoods finally aired yesterday. It was exciting. I thank You for the opportunity to make and to celebrate Chicago neighborhoods.

And I thank You, too, for my career as a novelist which has kept me from slipping into a rut as I grow older. Life may be exhausting now but it surely isn't dull. Better, much better, the former than the latter.

November 16

I QUOTE from a new Irish magazine called *Alpha*. Brother Mark Patrick Hederman, an Irish teacher, says: "He's very like a wealthy and important person who has fallen in love with a call girl . . . we're just not interested in God as a lover. We're just very pleased to take what's on offer and that is love. Love of God is something for which our culture and our civilization has no time."

"I feel very sorry for him," Brother Mark Patrick continues, "because in many situations I feel that His initial project, to win people to himself without any coercion, is really a fool's madness."

Sounds shocking? But Brother Mark Patrick is merely echoing here the Book of Hosea.

In the first answer, the goodness of God is put in question. In the second, God's power. In either case we have mystery, but I would rather put the mystery in God's vulnerability than in God's insensitivity. Both answers, be it noted, are well within the boundaries of orthodoxy.

Brother Mark Patrick again (as quoted in *Alpha*): "At the level of Creator, God is all powerful but the great mystery is that at the level of lover He is our equal if not our inferior because he won't employ the tricks and cruelties that we employ . . . God's loving is in the modality of vulnerability . . . we are God's equals at the level of loving and that's a huge responsibility for anybody who is a lover."

November 17

I'M back down to earth at last, more or less, and reasonably caught up on my work. I suppose I'll be fine by Monday and then I'll have to leave for Seattle and eight more hours in an airplane. I'm not sure why I get myself into these things.

Fortunately I experienced rather little depression this time around, although there are a lot of events just now that might depress me. Perhaps I have learned with Your help not to care about them.

The quotes from Brother Mark Patrick that I wrote down yesterday are fascinating, are they not? *Alpha* presented them as radical, though I'm not sure why the prophet Hosea should be considered all that innovative or radical! Still I suppose that we have ignored those images for so long that when we hear them they seem new and original.

How tedious it must be for You to have been so systematically misunderstood.

All I add to his imagery is the poignancy of imagining You as womanly. That makes the image even more provocative and powerful. You are like a vulnerable woman who needs to be protected from disreputable and exploitive lovers, of which I am surely one.

I don't grasp fully myself the enormity of that image. I suppose I never will, even though I try my best in these notes to imagine in that context. It will take a while before I'm ready to preach it in any but the most cautious way—save perhaps in poetry which has the merit of bemusing and confusing the literalists completely.

On the level of creation You are indeed the Lord (or Lady) of the Universe. On the level of relationship You are subject to my rejection and needing my loving care.

Help me to understand better the meaning of this mystery. I believe it intellectually. It has yet to transform my life.

November 18

THE gospel today has more stories of Jesus healing; the Evangelist is driving home his point that Jesus came to heal, that we who follow him are healed, and that we must also heal others.

Tired as I am from the jet lag and the other discontents of plane travel—and faced with a cross-continent flight the day after tomorrow, it is hard to feel healed and to feel that one has the resources to heal. Is there ever a

time in life when one doesn't feel tired? I can't remember
it.

I can act like a healer when I feel healed, physically,
mentally, emotionally. When I don't feel on top of the
world it is difficult for me to heal others. Self-preoccupation, I guess. There is so much to do there doesn't seem
to be any time for healing or for the kind of reflection
that is required to feel healed.

I'm still not making much sense. I'm sorry. I know You
love me and will always love me. I know with Brother
Mark Patrick that You depend on my love, as pathetic
as it is. I do love You, even if I'm too battered just now
to do much of a job expressing it.

November 20

THERE are advantages in being God.

Yesterday I reported that my post-travel depression had
become serious. I'm afraid that in the course of the day
it became acute—and myself, as the Irish would say, flying to Seattle today.

I'll really be a basket case by the end of the week. I
suppose, as I said yesterday, that I ought to take time
off after an overseas trip. It always seems to end up that
there is something to do right before I leave and right
after I come home. More careful planning would avoid
that situation and I'll try in the future to do that.

Yet physical weariness and depression are part of the
human condition. I accept them as indications of my fini-
tude and mortality and tell You that I love You and I

know You love me no matter how down I am. There are the usual aggravations that go with the territory of what I am and what I do. My reaction to them these last few days is the problem. Yet I must be patient with my reaction, knowing that it will go away in another week or so and I'll be OK again.

Even in these words I am perhaps too hard on myself, not as tolerant of my own frailty as You would be. Or as You in fact are.

In the gospel these days, Jesus is talking about the difficulty of being a follower of his. Why should I expect that it would be easy for me and that I would be an exception to this rule? On the one hand I must be patient with my own limitations and on the other realistic about what the world is like.

Anyway, I'm still wandering, I fear. Take care of me for the rest of this week. I love You.

And I know You need to hear that from me as much, no, more than I need to say it.

Seattle, November 21

A DARK, cloudy, typical Seattle day.

Nice night yesterday with Archbishop Tom Murphy and his friends. People here actually think I have something to say. That's one of the great advantages of being from out of town.

A Mass this morning at which the local good shepherd nuns renewed their vows on this feast of Mary, the Mother of Jesus. It was a touching ceremony and kind of sad. The nuns are half old and half late middle-age. No young ones anymore.

I look at the old faces and the bent bodies and picture them as young women, upright and intense, taking their vows for the first time—filled with enthusiasm and dedication. Now they see their community slowly dying. They must not regret their commitments or they would have left with the others. But how do they feel about the changes? How do they react to the death of the order to which they dedicated their lives? How do they feel about the repudiation by the Church of much of what they thought they once stood for?

I think we let these women down.

You love them of course and You are grateful for their commitment to special service for You and that is finally what counts. You will take care of them and make them young again and dry their tears and heal their wounds, as You will for all of us.

So my sadness for them is not so much misplaced as short-run. In the end, You will make all things well.

Seattle, November 22

I'M in the United red carpet room at 6:30 Seattle time waiting for a plane back to Chicago on the busiest travel day of the year. O'Hare at high noon on Thanksgiving Eve should be an interesting experience.

Take care of and protect all those traveling today and also guard them from the ill temper and edginess which often ruins family reunions in this supposedly joyous season.

The joyous season begins today, doesn't it? I mean in fact, if not in liturgical theory. So when I go home from Grand Beach on Sunday I'll have to get out my Christmas tree and my Christmas tapes and begin my Christmas shopping on Monday. After next week's pilgrimage to Ann Arbor there will be, thank God, no more plane trips till I go to Tucson and no more big writing projects. I can concentrate on sociology, on getting ready for Christmas and slowing down the engine a little bit.

Or at least that's the plan. Help me to have an especially happy Christmas this year.

My talk was well received last night. I was impressed by the professionalism of the sponsoring school—the best I've ever seen.

I seem at last to be back on Chicago time which is an improvement, although I'm not over the depression effects of the transatlantic jaunt. I guess the warmth of my reception here and the appreciation for my work was like a shot in the arm. For that, much thanks.

Friday and Saturday at Grand Beach may be a time to get back in reasonably good shape. I thank You for the rejuvenation of last night. Protect me on this crazy, busy day.

November 23

IT started out as a relaxing morning of swimming and reading and reflection with no rush. Then somehow the usual rush to get organized for leaving the house intervened and now I've sat down at noon to write this journal entry and I'm in a rush snit. I wonder as I write this how many times I leave my apartment this way. Probably most of the time.

Why don't I get things organized beforehand so I won't have to rush? The answer is that the rush is in getting things organized. If I waited till the last minute to prepare to leave I'd never get to anything!

I suppose the solution might be to prepare even earlier, especially on days like this one when I'm juggling a lot of agenda.

Anyway, I'll have to try to settle down before I leave.

The real solution is to curtail some of the activities. But then, I respond, "Hey, I've been away for two weeks and I'm only trying to catch up."

I always seem to be trying to catch up.

Maybe I can relax a bit at Grand Beach these next two days. I hope so.

Well, enough of this. It is Thanksgiving Day and I wish to be grateful for all that You've given me—beginning with my life which has been an invitation to a love affair with You. The time of that life is running out and I'm grateful for all the excitement and challenge and opportunity with which You have blessed me and also for the people whom I've loved and who have loved me. I'm a very fortunate person. I know that. I haven't been a grateful enough person. I know that too and I'm sorry.

Or rather I've tried to express my gratitude by doing when that is only part of the appropriate response and the less important part. I have been much less responsive by the more important way—loving You and reflecting on Your goodness as it breaks through the veils of creation all around me. I know in my heart that doing isn't enough, but a lifetime of habits are hard to change.

I promise in the next year to continue to try to change them.

Help me to love You more so I can be more grateful to You.

November 24

THIS is one of those days when it is very difficult to get started. However it is the last day of catching up—foolish, foolish phrase, isn't it?

The day is cold but beautiful. It's nice to be back at Grand Beach. Oddly enough, or perhaps not so oddly, this is still home.

I'm going to try to finish finishing up and then go for a walk this afternoon.

November 25

I FEEL drained as I did yesterday, not weary so much as recharging. I wish I could stay here at Grand Beach for a week instead of going back tomorrow. Yet I love Mass at St. Mary of the Woods and don't want to miss it. If I had been smart I'd have not scheduled it for this Sunday.

Enough on the subject of schedules. My real challenge during the month between today and Christmas is to prepare for Your Son's coming in all His different manifestations. Help me to do that, to reflect on the coming of the New Humanity and to take strength and courage from that coming, in which I believe so strongly but do not honor so often in practice.

November 26

BACK in Chicago to watch (on TV) the Bears blow another. Pathetic.

Not a fit subject for prayer!

I've put up the Christmas decorations and have the carols playing on hammered dulcimer and tomorrow I begin my Christmas shopping.

And I'm going to see *Prancer* tonight because I want to break, as best I can, the cycle of work and because it was made in Three Oaks.

The Christmas spirit begins early for me this year. I look forward to the joys of the season with some confidence that this year I can avoid the forces that seem to blot it out for me as we rush towards Christmas. Next weekend with the flight to Detroit will be difficult, but after that I propose to have fun and to celebrate this year.

I'll try to think of You often and to understand that this is the time of the year when You are most hungry for our love and are not likely to get it because we are so busy with so many things.

What do You want in the way of love from us? What do You need? What must You have? It's odd to put the question that way, but if I had not started to keep this journal I never would have discovered the implications of the vulnerability of God—Your vulnerability.

That's a question which should preoccupy me as the

days ahead develop—what does God need and want from us?

Love, surely. Concern, of course. Commitment, naturally.

Yet I find myself thinking that any lover wants attention. In the absence of attention how does the lover know that she is loved?

God wants our attention?

How can I escape the conclusion that You do?

Prayer is paying attention to God. Will that suffice as a tentative definition?

I think so.

November 27

THICK fog and rain all around my apartment, but Christmas lights inside amid dulcimer music and warmth. In the tenth chapter of Matthew's Gospel this morning we seem to have two sets of contrary sayings from Your son—who is, to be perfectly candid about it, given to saying things that seem contrary not to say contradictory. On the one hand he says that he has come not to bring peace but the sword and on the other that those who give a cup of water in His name will receive their reward.

He might well have added that those who seek to give a cup of water in His name will sometimes end up with the sword aimed at them.

I don't think it's a way out of the contradiction to say that the reward will come in the next life. Sure it will, but that is not, I am sure, what Himself meant.

Serving others in His name and Yours is a reward in

itself, not because it makes You feel good and generous but because generosity itself enhances and perfects the human spirit.

That reward is there even if those who resent You or hate You want to put You down and even destroy You. If You serve others in Jesus' name there will surely be both conflict and reward and that is the nature of the human condition as it currently exists.

As the mayor said to me on Saturday when I told him about yet another demonstration aimed at his alleged insensitivity, "It goes with the job."

Precisely. So it goes with the job of following Himself, however imperfectly I may do it. You're going to get clobbered, even perhaps by those who claim to be doing the same thing.

It goes with the job. If You don't like the heat, get out of the kitchen.

November 28

I'M so filled with renewed energy that I'm rearranging my apartment, putting it back in order again. Nothing like that for stirring up memories of the past and the frailty and the transiency of all things human.

A lot of failures, for my own blame in which (never easy to know precisely) I am sorry.

It's also an occasion of renewed sadness for those who have crossed the path of my life who are unhappy or suffering now. I wish to pray especially for them that they might find peace and joy. One or two of them, I hear rumors, are about to make a move to straighten out their lives. Help them to make it, whether they come back to my love or not.

I'm sorry for the ways I might have messed up with them in my desperate attempts to save them from what happened in their lives.

Maybe I should have prayed for them more in line with my reflections yesterday about Your liking to have attention. So I'm sorry for that. I'll try to pray for them more often in the days ahead.

November 29

IT's the feast of Saint Andrew.

In a few minutes I'm off to Quigley Seminary to say Mass, a nostalgia trip if there ever was one. I often walk by it now, only a half block away, and hardly remember that I once went through its doors for five years—and rarely in the last thirty, never in the last fifteen.

Last night Bishop Kaffer had a dinner in my honor out in Clarendon Hills (I didn't realize it was in my honor till I got there) with my classmates and contemporaries. Lots of memories, some pleasant, some less so. They are all, by their own admission, old. They feel old and look old. I don't feel old and don't look old either—most of that is genetic luck, a little bit is exercise, and the rest is the result of the new challenges You brought into my life in the last decade.

For all of these I'm very grateful indeed. Help me to make good use of the energy and vitality with which You have blessed me.

The energies are particularly strong now, which made the contrast last night more striking.

I don't know where they came from or how long they'll last. Maybe it's the sunny weather or getting over the jet lag from Ireland, but I'm filled with drive again, like it was the end of the summer.

I'll try to pay attention to You, as my lover who wants and needs my attention as I rush around, caught up in the smell and the sound and the color of Christmas.

Help those whom I love who are sick or troubled or lonely at this time of the year.

Again, thank You for the challenges in my life and the vitality with which to respond.

December 1

NOVEMBER is over, a busy month, an exciting month, an exhausting month. I have a feeling of frustration that I accomplished so little, a silly reaction but typical of my achievement-oriented life. It was a good month and I thank You for it and its challenges and rewards. Take care of me in this new month. Grant that the energy and serenity that I have now may persist through the Christmas time and beyond.

Help me also to give You the attention that as a lover You need and want from me. I seriously wonder about Your taste in lovers and friends, but there's no point in trying to argue with You on that subject.

I'm off to Ann Arbor today for the weekend, usually an exhausting experience because I don't travel well and

Andrew Greeley

I endure overnights outside of hotels even less well. Is it a sign of age, I wonder, to be such a difficult traveler?

I was that way, as You well know, when I was thirty! I therefore expect points from You for my courage in traveling.

All right, I know our relationship isn't about points.

It's nice to be back at Grand Beach. Oddly enough, or perhaps not so oddly, this is still home.

So a story like last night's opera expresses the human hope for happy endings and a fixer who will guarantee such endings. Who is to say that such an evening is not finally more revelatory than my weekend visit to a friend who will surely die soon. We will all live happily ever after.

Eventually.

As we know from Mozart's opera everything is not always perfect between Rosina and the count.

But Figaro takes care of that too, doesn't he?

Perhaps You are indeed Figaro!

December 6

I WILL sing of the Lord's kindness forever, says the psalmist in today's reading. What a wonderful idea! Singing forever of Your kindness! Isn't that what a human life should be—a song of praise? The psalmist talks of natural and communal blessings, You delivered his people from their oppressors, You knocked off Rahab and the other sea monsters, You bring the rains which water the crops.

All of these are very clever and very benign events.

Thanks to the Hebrew prophets, however, we now think of Your interpersonal kindness too, Your loving concern for each one of us, even to return to an earlier metaphor, the little baby that cries. The delicacy of Mary for Your son and hers in the crib scene is a symbol of Your kindness for each of us, a kindness so overwhelming that it is hard to credit, a kindness which will make all right in the end no matter what happens in life.

When I look at my life I am astonished at the kindness of Your concern—so many, many good things, so many surprises and delights, so many loves old and new. I don't know what I have done to deserve such an exciting and rewarding life. Or rather I know that I have done nothing at all to deserve it. Everything is a pure gift of Your kindness for which all I can do is say thanks and promise to respond to the gifts, however ineptly and crudely, with love and generosity—and songs of praise!

My song, I fear, has often been off-key and dull. Let it not be that way in however many days remain to me.

Let me sing more brightly and cheerfully and happily each day of Your kindness and all the days of my life, especially in this joyous season.

December 7

PEARL HARBOR day, the day the world changed forever. Grant rest and peace to all those who died in the war and to those who still live and are haunted by its memories. And thank You for the final ending of the war—or so it seems—in Eastern Europe.

Today's gospel reading tells of the demand on Jesus

for a miracle and his firm rejection of the demand. It fits nicely with the reading from Joseph Nozick who points out wisely that signs and miracles, no matter how great, cannot confirm the existence of God save for those who already believe and want confirmation.

The signs of Your presence are all around us—in the sun which is just rising, in the clear blue sky, in the city spread out in front of me from my window, in the Christmas lights and and trees and gifts in my apartment, in the friends I will see and talk to during the day.

Or, on a more abstract level, creation is the biggest sign of all, the largest miracle of all. If it doesn't persuade no lesser sign will persuade. If the mystery of why there is anything doesn't awe us, then no lesser mystery can conceivably create awe.

As I write these words I am awed by the waking city around me and my waking life. Unfortunately I get so caught up in the daily demands of that life I forget that I live immersed in and pervaded by mystery. Wonder is not in Yugoslavia where folks are running these days for signs; wonder is here now (which is not to say that I reject their devotion). I am steeped in it, surrounded by it, intimate with it.

Help me to keep in touch with wonder and mystery during the day and every day. Let me see the lights on the tree and the large candles in the window as explosive signals of wonder each time I come into the apartment.

December 8

A FEAST in honor of the Mother of Jesus who is the best hint we have of Your maternal womanly love and of Your vulnerability and need for our loving and responsive attention.

It is yet another day to ponder wonder and surprise. I read this morning a story about alchemy and a young man who worked long hours, days and months on his banana plantation to accrue the silver dust necessary to turn base metal into gold. Sure enough, his wife sold the bananas he discarded in his search for gold and made a lot of gold for the family, not through magic but through hard work.

I would interpret this story as meaning that the greatest fantasy of all exists not in the arena of magic and imagination but rather in the magical and fantastical events of daily life and love.

We enter the world of story not to stay there, not because we think it is more real than ordinary life, but to acquire the vision to be able to see the fantasy and magic of real life more clearly. Story listening is designed to give us eyesight into the fantastical and the magical all around us.

Just like I saw Lincoln Park for the first time through the lens of Tony Bill's camera in *My Bodyguard* and Three Oaks, Michigan, through the cameraman's eye in *Prancer* and much of the beauty of Chicago when I was taking pictures for my book about the city.

There is alchemy in organizing a mass of data into a coherent report, in recapturing an old and lost love, in decorating a Christmas tree, in picking the right presents for the right people, in telling a story which captivates small children.

We are a magic-making, alchemizing species. I perform miracles every day (sometimes it's almost a miracle that I get out of bed in the morning!) and do wondrous things all through the day—all too often without realizing that because activities are common, even commonplace, it does not follow that they are mundane.

We are the only species of which we know that can perform wonders and we do so routinely. If the angels are better than us at the wonder game (and I suppose they are), they have to be very wonder-full indeed.

I suspect that often You are astonished at how we permit our magical abilities to becoming BORING!, how we permit routine to eliminate our sense of the marvelous spells and tricks we perform with ease.

Help me to be more alive to the wonder that exists not only outside my self, but in the depths of my personality and in the ordinary (so-called) skills of our species.

December 9

MY BELOVED,

Shea and I saw *Steel Magnolias* yesterday (but not *The Little Mermaid* which I must still see). It was a multiple handkerchief (or should I say tissues these days?) film, but with an enormously thoughtful religious theme (implicit, but barely, with the final scene being on Easter and emphasizing children as symbolizing the triumph of life over death).

YEAR OF GRACE

It did assume that women are superior to men which neither You nor I would be inclined to dispute—and oddly enough it was not written by a woman. More to the point of these reflections, it depicted powerfully the heartache of life, of relations between husband and wife, parents and children, and of death, expected and unexpected, early and not so early.

At first I thought that its theme was the exact opposite to my reflections of the last couple of days about humans as a wonder species. However that was an early and erroneous reaction. In fact it portrayed the greatest wonder of them all—our ability to transcend death and to renew love, surely the most astonishing kind of magic that one could imagine.

Surely that ability is the most powerful hint we have of Your presence in the world, mourning with us, transcending death with us, renewing love with us. And it is a promise that together there is no suffering, no pain, no heartache which together we cannot in the long run overcome. As I have said before the mystery is the difference between Your short-run performances and long run, the former leading to Woody Allen's comment that You are an underachiever. I don't understand the mystery but that's where I want to put the mystery.

All the people in the film will die eventually as did the young mother. So all of us die eventually. I will die eventually too, in the not too distant future in all probability. Yet no human experience of love is ever forgotten in Your mind, as the process theologians say. So the young mother's love of her own mother, her husband, and her child are not forgotten. So my loves are not forgotten.

And if the love survives surely the lover must survive

too. That finally is what faith means, is it not? How You are going to work it out, I don't know, but then if I did understand You, You would not be God would You?

The poignancy and the mystery—and the wonder—of the human condition is that we know all of these things simultaneously, as sure as we know that we live. We may say it awkwardly as did the Darryl Hannah character in the film, but we don't doubt it in the depths of our soul even if at times we reject that certainty.

So thanks for the film, which is fine preparation for Christmas.

December 10

MY BELOVED,

Is it really true, the poet John Betjamin asks in the Christmas poem which I found yesterday and did not bring to St. Mary of the Woods to read. (Better next week anyway). Is the core story of Christmas really true?

He doesn't mean truth in the literal details, the kind on which the fundamentalists fixate. He means rather the theologial truth of the Incarnation. Again the issue isn't one of definitions, not whether Chalcedon is a precise description of the relationship between humanity and divinity in Your son Jesus.

Rather the question is whether God (Yourself!) loved us so much as to take on human flesh (in whatever fashion) so as to share our life, our suffering, and our death with us.

It was a dazzling notion then and it still is, however much it may have been obscured by obscure theological debates and obscure heresy hunters. For if it is true, the Bethlehem story, then the world is a wonderful, magical place filled with dizzying possibilities for joy and surprise.

We celebrate it wildly this time of the year and, as Betjamin's poem says, a lot of the celebration seems to have little to do with the Bethelem event. Indeed many of the vignettes in the book are all about Christmas and not at all about Christ. I think of Washington Irving and Dylan Thomas on the details of the celebration and not a reference to what was being celebrated. Or the necessarily insincere, painted-smile holiday best wishes on TV.

On the other hand I don't want to exclude an honest if dimly perceived link between the celebrations of the next two weeks (lunch and supper for me every day from now on) and what happened in Bethlehem. Men and women are celebrating light in darkness, renewal, rebirth, new life even if they don't quite grasp the religious, not to say the theological, details.

There are, as You well know, sacraments all over the place this time of the year. We who are sacrament makers and celebrators should seize on every one we can and illumine them even more.

We have to see them ourselves, of course. I must realize that the lights along the Magnificent Mile are You and Your Son, the light of the world. That the big Christmas tree, quite beautiful really, in front of my building is the link between heaven and earth, the axis mundi, the fertilization of the sky by the earth.

And the light came into the darkness and the darkness was not able to put it out!

Andrew Greeley

December 11

ONLY two weeks till Christmas. All my shopping done. In better spirits and health than I have been at this time of the year for many years. For which, many, many thanks. God (You) grant that I continue that way.

In the poem I read yesterday by Richard Wilbur he says that a thing only becomes most itself when it is likened: a metaphor makes a reality more fully real than it is before. Surely that is the case with You. When I use metaphors to talk to You and about You I know You much better. The image of You as a woman and a vulnerable woman does make You more Yourself for me.

It also makes me understand the vulnerability of women better when I see them in You and You in them. Which is what metaphor is supposed to do.

Alas, the metaphor is only beginning to change my life, and that slowly. No, that's not the way I want to say it. What I mean is that I accept the metaphor, rejoice in it, revel in it, but it does not fully permeate my being.

But that way it sounds absurd doesn't it? I know enough about human nature and about metaphors to understand that the effect of the latter on the former is slow, subtle, and irresistible. A metaphor is not supposed to work overnight. I must be patient as it has its effect on me and remain open to the effect.

Which is I guess what I really want to say. I'm not yet as open to the effect of the metaphor of the vulnerability of God as a "shy child" as I would want to be.

I think I can get away with that assertion and not be demanding too much of either You or me.

160

Hence I can pray this lovely Advent time that I may become ever more open to the metaphor with which I pray to You each day and let it slowly transform my life.

December 12

JOSEPH NOZICK in the book I am reading currently says that faith is trust in Your own deepest experience. At first this seems a minimalist regard for You—except that ingenious seducer that You are You disclose Yourself most fully in our deepest experiences. They are the place where we encounter You. All the religion, all the theology, all the catechisms in the world are merely explications of and deductions from descriptions of such experiences. Thus my current reflections on You as a loving and vulnerable woman are nothing more than my attempt to describe and explicate who and what You are—or perhaps more accurately who and what You are like.

Religious langauge is metaphor for these deepest experiences. Religious faith is trust in them. A religious life is a life in tune with the directions which seem to emerge from them. You are the One who is encountered, mysteriously, attractively, enchantingly in the deepest moments of those experiences.

Everything else is added on.

The experiences are of course shaped by the traditions from which we spring. You are surely a result in my imagination of the images of the Mother of Jesus which I have seen from chilhood, both a lover and a mother or a lover who is a mother as well as a vulnerable lover.

The issue is how far we can trust these experiences, how far trust the lover encounter in the depths of the richest moments of our life. No one, You should excuse the expression, trusts You completely. Very few are able, on the other hand, to doubt You totally, despite their efforts to do so.

We want proof. Nozick neatly dismisses that by saying, isn't the sun a proof? It doesn't have to dance as it is alleged to have done at Fatima; existence up there is wonder enough (even on days like today when it just barely appears above the horizon, maybe especially on these days because we know it will come back next week). It is not Your fault that we don't know You better. It is in the nature of things.

The question, the mystery, the enchantment too, is the question of who the hell are You really. We only get whiffs of You in the wonder experiences, powerful whiffs indeed, but then You are gone, like Ariel, the little mermaid.

That, too, is in the nature of things, I guess. You reveal as much of Yourself as You can.

To trust in those wonder experiences is to cling to the precipice of meaning as we hang suspended over the abyss of chaos.

I continue to cling. I would do no other.

Help me to know You better.

December 13

I DON'T mind cold winter mornings like this one on which it is difficult to get a start on both the car and my work. I mind the snow on the ground, especially when I must go somewhere every night on slippery streets. I think, with all due respect, that it's the snow on the streets which is unacceptable.

Oh well. In Your wisdom You have sent me off to Arizona in the winter. So I'm much better off than most Chicagoans—though if I had my choice (which in this matter You haven't really given me) I'd rather be here. On days like this—snow on the ground and more coming and temperature below ten degrees all day—I begin to count the days till Tucson.

Anyway, despite the cold and the snow, Chicago looks beautiful out my window this morning, light and pastel like a Impressionist Christmas card—a nice preparation for Christmas. Hence I am content with the modest proposal that there not be too much snow this afternoon when I go over to Holy Family for supper.

Nozick has a wonderful chapter in his book on the holiness of every day in which he suggests we touch the holiness of things by enjoying their taste, feel, smell, sound. In particular he emphasizes the taste of food as something to be savored and enjoyed to the fullest (all the while admitting with becoming modesty that he doesn't do it very well himself). If one wants to encounter You in the ordinary (which is what holiness is—Your presence) one must be sensitive to the wonders of the ordinary, which means the taste of food, to which I pay so little attention.

This is the time of the year when one must eat—and at the same time talk, activities which if the truth be told are not always compatible. Last night's supper was wondrous. I knew the food tasted good. I even complimented my hostess more than I would have if I were only being polite. As a matter of fact, now remembering the night before, I did the same thing then. Yet I can't say that I reveled in the marvelous taste of the food the way I would have if I were thinking about them as sacraments of Your presence, as they are. I talk sacramentality a lot and maybe practice it sometimes, but I gulp food down (not as quick as does my friend the Mayor) with all too little attention to the sheer marvel of flavor. BAD!

Take raspberries for example. As You well know I take exception to the limitation You impose on the season in this part of the world. I assume that in the World-to-Come You will have a year long season for them. Nonetheless, while I enjoyed the raspberry salad and the raspberry desert last night (undoubtedly both put together because of my obsession with them!) I never did savor their taste as I might have if I had given it a few seconds extra thought.

I'll have them at lunch again today at the Tavern Club and I promise that I'll try to enjoy them as one of the wonders of Your creation. I hope I can grow in this minor awareness of the holiness of things, of Your presence in them.

Raspberries are the thing with which to start, that's for sure.

Apricot cookies too. And oatmeal raisin.

The list could grow long.

Maybe tomorrow I'll put down the full list, or better yet, the Christmas list.

December 14

No raspberries at the Tavern Club! Very funny!

But I did savor some other things. Not much, though. I'll keep trying.

Despite that I had a very interesting experience after lunch yesterday, the closest thing to a mystical interlude ever in my life. Not really mystical, not like the sort of thing on which I've done sociological research, but still a hint of what those encounters with You must be like.

I was riding down the escalator at Fields after buying some picture frames on the eighth floor. I turned at the mezzanine and saw the first floor spread out in all its Christmas splendor, thronged with people. For just an instant I understood everything—Christmas, life, death, the human condition—and all fit together in one splendid harmony.

Like an idiot, I didn't stop to reflect or to enjoy, but I rushed on with my chores and my work. Yet the memory lingers and perhaps always will. I'll go back there and try to plumb it more thoroughly, perhaps write a poem about it.

I'm sure my reflections in this journal about deep experiences made me open to it, but what an odd and unusual and wonderful place for it to happen. I'm also sure that my approach to Christmas this year, more peaceful and relaxed thus far anyway, also helped.

I'm going to proclaim a moratorium on work starting either Saturday or Sunday to prepare more for Christmas.

Thank You for that brief encounter yesterday. I'm sorry

if I made it too brief. I'll go back and see if You're still there.

Of course You will be because You are everywhere. And I can find You everywhere if I have the eyes to see and the ears to hear.

I'll do the list of Christmas tastes tomorrow, except I want to list chocolate chip cookies now.

December 15

INSTEAD of sitting down in front of this machine after my swim this morning I watched the video of *Babette's Feast* which came in yesterday's mail, as preparation for the article I am writing for *America* on the Eucharist. What a wonderful vision of food and drink as sacrament—from Isak Dinesen of all people and in the atmosphere of Danish pietism at that.

How little we Catholics really understand the Eucharist as sacrament—as a reflection of both the heavenly banquet (at which, as one of the sisters says at the end of the story, Babette will delight the angels) and of our ordinary human eating and drinking. In conjunction with the passage from Nozick I read earlier in the week about the holiness of food, Babette's Feast has made this a special week—food as wonder experience, food as revelation, food as source of depth experience, food as a hint (as the general says at the end of the film) that in this beautiful world of ours all things are possible.

I must try to integrate this rich insight into my Christmas eating and also in my writing and story telling.

Thank You for the insight and the illumination. Help me not to forget it.

And tomorrow I absolutely promise that I'll give the list of Christmas delights, adding right after chocolate chip cookies anything with apricot flavor!

December 16

ONLY one more article to write—and that before the day is over—and I will declare my Christmas moratorium on work. It will be a relief.

This morning I finished an introduction to the anthology of science fiction stories with some kind of Catholic theme in them. It is an incredibly rich collection—more of the analogical imagination at work. I am grateful for being part of the tradition of that imagination.

Now to be fully analogical, my list of delightful Christmas tastes. I restate chocolate chip cookies and anything with apricot taste. Also those little crumbly cookies with powdered sugar, turkey stuffing (without the turkey, please!) fruit cake, plum pudding (easy on the whiskey!), eggnog, cranberries, the fondue hat trick at the Hornadays (Christmas by association), all other kinds of cookies, Bailey's Irish Cream (not limited to Christmas, of course!), champagne (in very limited amounts), Christmas candy, especially if it has raspberry flavors, cinnamon rolls for breakfast and also coffee cake!

My mouth waters as I go through the list—and my stomach prepares to revolt!

It's not quite the outburst of "A Child's Christmas in

Wales" and I'm surely not Dylan Thomas, poor dear man. But You get the point: I am grateful indeed for those wonderful manifestations of Your goodness that are available to me at Christmastime. I rejoice in them as a revelation of You and Your love. I promise to try to enjoy them more fully this year than ever before, to savor their taste, to revel in their goodness, and to think often of how they reflect a heavenly banquet which will be even more sumptuous.

So far, despite the cold weather and my work load, I'm more atuned to Christmas than I have been since I was a child. That's a great grace and one for which I am very thankful. I hope this week to come to pray and reflect more and perhaps write some poetry about this season when, despite the darkness, Your light seems to shine everywhere.

December 17

LATE Sunday evening and the first chance I have had to get to this journal. I'm caught up in the Christmas rush with little time now to reflect on it. I must make more serious efforts tomorrow to reassert some kind of control. The problem is that my best way this year to keep control has been the morning swim and the morning journal entry. I got the swim in this morning but not the journal entry because I had to hurry to get up to St. Mary of the Woods for Mass. The result has been a disorganized and disorderly day. I didn't have the time because the dinner was late last night and I needed more sleep this morning—a vicious circle if You will. It seems that every time I leave the apartment these days I am, a) leaving in a rush and b) leaving something behind for which I must return.

This simply has to stop. It means, I suppose, not cutting the times of departure as close as I do—and not answering the phone when it rings while I am preparing to depart. I am sorry to have to bother You with these essentially silly problems, but, alas, they are a part of my spiritual life and I must reflect on them.

As I'm sure You know, my lack of reflection on the problems of the Church is not the result of an absence of concern. Rather I feel that there is little I can do that I'm not already doing with my columns and my novels.

Help me to do what I should do in the present circumstances.

December 18

MY DEAR ONE,

A week before Christmas—and the orgy of eating and drinking continues. I guess the only thing to do is to enjoy it and try to be as moderate as possible without offending hostesses. Incidentally, I made a grave mistake of omission in my list of Christmas delights: I forgot oatmeal raisin cookies!

Two chilling stories in Matthew this morning: Jesus being thrown out of Nazareth and John the Baptist being beheaded—both exercises of envy.

December 19

THE COLD wave continues unabated into its second week with a promise of 30 below before this week is over. Most inconsiderate of You at Christmas time!

A lot about death in my reading this morning: Nozick reflects on dying, Wilbur's poem about the death of W.H. Auden and the death of all of us. But Wilbur also writes about the return of the trees in spring and in the gospel Jesus feeds the multitude, men and women hungry for food and for life.

As I look out the window today, snow flurries falling, clouds low and threatening, frozen smoke rising from the buildings, I can't question the reality of death—even if my doctor yesterday said I was glowing with health (for which in passing much thanks!). Only a few more years and it will all be over.

What difference will all the battles fought and lost and the few fought and won make?

The crib scene I guess is the answer to that. Birth is stronger than death. At Bethlehem Your love established a "we" relationship (which is what Nozick very rightly calls love) between Yourself and us, between You and me. That link can never be resolved. All my efforts, no matter how trivial and how imperfect, are still caught up in that link and preserved forever in Your mind and heart.

So I should look beyond the grayness outside and see the light, look beyond the frozen trees and see the green again of spring.

The light penetrates the darkness and the darkness cannot put it out. The warmth breaks through into the cold and the cold cannot dim its fire. Love fractures death and death cannot be put back together again.

Finally this is not a reasoned position. It is a leap into a link of love which You established when You created me and which Christmas confirms, validates, and solidifies.

Your son fed the multitude and thus promised them life, and by so doing confirmed the implicit promise which exists already in our emergence as a reflective species. Here again the "deepest" experiences manifest themselves. Christmas is the story which most perfectly tells of that deep experience and confirms my deepest hopes.

So let it be cold!

I really don't mean that as You well know. Let it be warm, please. Or warmer anyway. But if for reasons that escape me it has to be cold then there will be enough warmth in the Christmas story, more than enough, for a lifetime.

December 20

THE solstice approaches and the weather gets colder. The meteorologists say that You intend to warm things up a bit by Christmas which would be most gracious. No one seems to want to slow down the holiday rush because of the cold weather, which proves something even if I don't know what.

We invaded Panama this morning. More bodies for Christmas.

Andrew Greeley

We receive Steve Neal into the Church this morning, an altogether joyous event, for which thanks.

The poem from Wilbur this morning is a translation of Mirabeau Bridge by Apollinaire:

All love goes by as water to the sea
All love goes by
How slow life seems to me
How violent the hope of love can be.

How violent the hope of love can be! What powerful words! And how true. I have often argued that love is not sweet or nice or lace and flowers but a wild and fearsome energy compelling us towards union. The ultimate hope of love, as Nozick notes in his essay on dying today, is union after death, as fierce a passion as exists in the human condition, although some would deny it's pertinence, mostly I think because they deceive themselves.

Love flows by, life flows by, the water seems to move slowly, though sometimes, oh so rapidly. And all the time love draws and pushes, leads and demands, enthralls and entrances, deprives us of our sanity and makes us more than human.

As I also have said before, how odd of You to claim to be Love.

And how wonderful!

The poet adds that "neither time past/nor love comes back again" under the Mirabeau Bridge.

Perhaps he should have read Proust. The past can be recreated in our memory by stories, and love, once forgotten, can be rekindled.

So too my love for You, weaker at some times than at others, can be reawakened.

A lot of the matters raised by the poem and by the essay are beyond my comprehension—and beyond anyone's as far as that goes. So I have to take the great leap of love into the Seine and go with the flow as the violent hope of love carries me through life.

December 21

A bright, bright day for the shortest one in the year—with wind chills of 35 below. I will not waste my time complaining about the weird behavior of the jet stream which has produced this weather. I presume it's one of those events for which You will disclaim short term responsibility. Always the same line—when good things happen You take the credit, when bad things happen You say that it's not Your fault.

All right, all right, I'm only kidding!

Steve's reception into the Church yesterday was a graceful event. He's clearly very happy about being a Catholic. I don't quite understand why yet—not why anyone would want to be a Catholic but why this particular person would want to be a Catholic. But he does and he's happy and so are his wife and kids so that's enough and more than enough.

Richard Wilbur's poem this morning about story telling and the little unexplained obscurities which are necessary for a good story is illuminating on this and the other mysteries of life. Stories must explain most things but they can't explain everything without losing some of their power—this despite those who want every loose end tied up. Life is filled with loose ends which will never be tied up, mysteries little and big which boggle the imagination when we think about them and which make life interesting and fascinating as background color. There are so many loose ends in my life, so very many. As I ponder them this Christmastime I can only ask You for forgiveness for my mistakes and guidance in those stories which are still open-ended.

This all sounds confused, I know. Maybe it's only the cold weather. What I'm trying to say is that I concede You the necessary loose ends in order that Your empirical and pragmatic providence may attain its goals. I even concede the fact that mysteries enhance life rather than detract from it. What I regret is the unnecessary loose ends that I have interjected into Your schemes— all the while knowing that You can turn them into grace.

I was a very minor actor in Steve's becoming a Catholic. I'm glad, however, that I could play that minor role.

December 22

I KNOW You love each single person who died in the square in Bucharest and everyone shot in the back in Panama, as much as You love me and more than any human lover could love them. I know You will take care of them and dry their tears and the tears of those who loved them. I know that in the long run, in Your time, they will live and love and laugh again. I believe that with all the power of my belief.

Yet as I watch the sunset in the western sky on this

cold, cold first full day of winter with the dulcimer tones of Christmas carols in the background and Christmas lights all around my apartment I mourn for them, people whom I have never met who are dying at Christmastime because of political absurdity, because of cruelty and stupidity, because of cowardice and fear.

Take them home with You and bring them peace. Bring peace to all the other lonely, frightened, confused, injured people in this world. Make Christmas somehow come true for all of them. And help me to realize how fragile a festival this is, how weak is all human hope— and how powerful as I said yesterday is all human love.

Bring peace on earth, Your peace, not only the peace which is to come, but even present peace. Thank You for all the wondrous, miraculous freedom in Eastern Europe. May the star shine over everyone. May Your kingdom come.

December 23

AS You remember I was complaining—tongue in cheek, about all the food and drink and especially about people who constrain me to eat chocolate chip cookies. I was also complaining about the Lent which will begin next year.

And I was adding (when I goofed up on the machine) that seriously these are glorious times even if one feels stuffed and tired. I thank You for all the loyal friends and family with which You've blessed me. Help me to continue to bring laughter and joy as I make my Christmas rounds. Thank You for enabling me to give many Christmas presents. Help me to realize that the coming of the Child, Your son, changed everything and that because of it I can face whatever is ahead, old age, disappointment, defeat, and death, with confidence that in the end all manner of things will be well.

And bring peace to both Panama and Romania this Christmas time.

Also consider said whatever I said before, which You remember even if my treacherous hard disk does not!

Noel!

December 24

MY LOVE,

Christmas Eve. The city is gray and cloudy and, Thank You Very Much, substantially warmer. There is a hint of snow in the sky, but only a light dusting, a white Christmas without any of the hassle. I'll accept that.

Something is still wrong with this machine. Now I don't get the collapsed display mode which is frustrating, though I think I have just figured out how to make it work again.

Anyway, this is a time of waiting, waiting for the night and the stars and the presents to be opened and the beginning of the day when, as Chesterton put it, the world was turned upside down and from this perspective suddenly looking right, the time when, as I have written in these reflections, we saw finally the ultimate pathos of God, the ultimate abandonment, the ultimate wonderment. God showing that S/He (You) suffer(s) with us. What a dizzying notion, one that I can barely grasp after all these years of celebrating Christmas, the ultimate gift, the ultimate hint, the final truth.

We would not, I think, have dared to suspect this on our own. Only because it has been revealed to us at Bethlehem and pondered over for so many years have we come to believe in it or perhaps I should say hope in it. That we dare to think it might be true is perhaps the best hint that we have that it is true.

This afternoon I am off to SMW to tell a story to the kids at the 4:30 Mass which in some respects seems to be replacing the midnight Mass as the high point of Christmas. Surely it is for those who have kids. I'll be back and perhaps make more entries in this journal after that event, which I love as much as the kids do.

Later.

The ceremony at SMW was wonderful! I think every kid in the parish was there, all filled with Christmas excitement. It was the kind of Eucharist that made one glad to be a Catholic—colorful, joyous, exuberant, exhilarating. I'm so grateful to You that I'm part of that parish. It's a wonderful place to be a priest and to have people that respond to me as a priest.

Also, the wide-eyed wonder of kids at Christmastime is pure sacrament. They're right about the marvel of the world. I do indeed believe they're right, even though I don't marvel nearly enough.

But thanks to You, I'm getting better at marveling. Merry Christmas! I'm sure the banquet in heaven at Christmastime is very special—and no worry about calories either!

Andrew Greeley

December 25

CHRISTMAS morning. The light has come into the world, or back into the world, and the world is filled with joy. I would imagine that You're petty happy too. Surely You ought to be: Christmas is one of Your better accomplishments. Many people today, I suppose, are not exactly sure what they're celebrating. Others know but are too busy to pay much attention to it (perhaps I will be in that latter category as the day goes on). Yet the very name of the feast recalls to mind a seemingly ordinary event in Palestine nineteen centuries ago which transformed human history and injected into the world an image of Your relationship with us that for almost blasphemous daring can never be topped.

Oh, yes, it's an impressive achievement, one that, as I reflected yesterday, it would take a God to figure out and achieve. It's not even God becoming human in Palestine as John Betjamin says, it's God becoming human so that S/He can suffer with us—really cry each time the baby cries. A couple of thousand years later we have not even begun to plumb the wonders of this mystery. Nonetheless it's well worth celebrating even if the precise reasons for the celebration are only dimly perceived by many of the celebrants.

These days are busy ones for me, not much time for contemplation or reflection which is all right, too, because they are the busy days of love and I do have time to write this journal and to pray occasionally. I hope when I come home this evening from my round of parties there'll be a few moments of quiet and peace to listen closely to carols and admire the light of the world and the mystery of joy, incredible joy, which breaks through at Christmastime.

December 26

ST. STEPHEN'S DAY

Last night after I came home from my Christmas rounds—delightful as always—as I sat in the chair, almost too tired to go to bed, I picked up the bound galleys of Mike Cizsintmihaly's new book on Flow. In some respects it's very disappointing. His work on the flow phenomenon is quite impressive and very helpful. But now, like a lot of men who have worked a long time on a research project, he is convinced that it is not only good research and helpful research but The Answer—that is, the answer to all human problems and the new religion. He has to pretty much dismissed on shallow grounds all previous religions to get away with this.

Delusions of grandeur, I'm afraid.

I know I don't have to tell You this because You've read the book already.

Nonetheless in his first chapter he addresses the question of happiness and asks how we pursue and obtain happiness. He suggests that we find happiness especially in response to challenge—a conclusion from his work with which I have no quarrel. He also says that the secret of happiness is to control our consciousness, which is true up to a point no doubt but does not follow from his research and tends in the direction of transcendental meditation and other similar foolish fads.

Andrew Greeley

Perhaps later I will return to this consciousness subject. Now I want to reflect on flow and happiness.

How can You be happy, I am often asked, with all the pressures that You experience because of the kinds of work You do. I've never taken it seriously as a question because it is at least sometimes a put down, an implication that it is unhappiness that drives me to the various things I do and to the many roles I play.

I like what I do, I usually reply. I don't want to give any of them up because I enjoy them. If I wear myself out or if my health slips and I have to give up something, then OK. Till then why not do the things that I enjoy doing, even if there are a lot of them?

That answer never seems to satisfy those who ask the question—in part I guess because the question isn't really a question at all but a sly criticism.

Last night for the first time I think I fully understoood why I am a very happy person: I like what I do; much of it is flow—the mix of challenge and achievement which is so pleasurable as to be an end in itself. The fun of writing a book or an article or a column is more important than the fun of actually seeing it published (though that is nice too).

This is a very great blessing and one for which I owe You enormous thanks.

It would be better perhaps, no certainly, if the flow wasn't almost addictive and I could take more time off to reflect and enjoy the other pleasures You have put in my life. But better to be addicted (or quasi-addicted) to flow activities than to have no flow at all, to be innocent of challenge and the response to challenge.

I now understand why pro athletes say that the game

is fun and they'll stop playing when it stops being fun. Despite the tremendous physical exertion and the pounding they take, the challenge and the response to challenge is indeed fun for them, too.

I am not sure how any of this came into my life— maybe the permeable boundaries about which I talked in my memoir. But it is a marvelous blessing for which I haven't thanked You nearly enough.

I should not feel guilty about working or enjoying my work, indeed reveling in it. I should devote more time to other matters and thus be able to enjoy the flow of challenge and response even more.

With Your help and Your love, I will try to do just that.

December 27

CAROL PHELAN died this morning. God (You) rest her. Death at Christmas—the worst time to die or the best? It is not fair that a young woman like her dies. It is not fair that anyone die. Why have You produced, very cleverly I would add, a creature that can reflect on its own mortality? Would it not be better if we were like the other animals and were unaware of our death—as we try to be much of the time?

You have created a being who longs not to die and then sentenced that being to death! Hardly seems right.

I know the answers and of course I accept them. You suffer with the bereaved, You mourn with the mourners, You grieve with those who grieve, You will eventually wipe away all tears, We shall all be young again, we shall all laugh again!

OK, I know those things. I accept the inevitability of my own death (grudgingly and with an attempt to avoid and repress the subject). I even accept the fact that Your plan must be beautiful and loving because that's what You are. I merely want to go on record as saying that it often doesn't look that way.

There is no good time to die. Some are just worse than others. There are no good ways to die. Some are just worse than others.

Carol died quickly which I suppose is good, though her family would have rather had her with them longer and she would have rather been with them longer. More suffering was avoided which is good, I guess; but there was no time for loving farewells.

Finally none of that matters. We die and that is that. Life looks like a brief interlude between two oblivions.

Obviously, I don't believe that, though I don't want to pretend that it is not a position which enjoys some plausibility.

All that is left then is faith in You and Your love, in the triumph of life over death we celebrate with Mary and Joseph at Bethlehem.

With all the hesitations and doubts that come with being human, I leap into that faith and trust in the power and goodness of Your love.

What else can I do?

December 29

I DON'T know what happened to yesterday. I guess I let myself be so caught up in my work that I forgot about everything else. Flow run out of control? The down side of the exuberance of responding to challenge?

Anyway, I'm sorry. I'm also sorry that I have somehow managed to become tired again. The energies of early December seem to have disappeared as quickly as they appeared. I'm sure the book I'm writing on fidelity is part of the problem. It consumes all my energy and time. I need to get to Arizona.

Even the film last night—*Family Business*—didn't produce the relaxing effect that films usually do. Too much work.

The conclusion is obvious. I should take the weekend off.

I took last week off didn't I?

Yeah, but it was Christmas week, hardly a time to relax.

OK, You win, like You always do. I'll abandon work tomorrow and Sunday.

And sleep late too.

December 30

INSTEAD of waiting till today, I took off yesterday. It was a good idea because I now feel fine again. Whatever else happens I should always swim first thing in the morning and write this journal second thing in the morning. While I don't believe in New Year's resolutions, I will nevertheless make that one now. The difference in my life when I begin the day with sound exercise of mind and body and when I don't is striking. I now have enough evidence from this semester so that the issue is beyond a doubt.

Andrew Greeley

The Phelan wake yesterday and the novels about young lovers which I have somehow been reading this last week are startling materials for reflection at the year's end. Dick and Carol were young lovers not so long ago. No, they were young lovers even this summer at Grand Beach. They were the kind of people who surely would have been in the "falling in love" category in my current research. How much we admire and honor young love and yet how quickly it passes — destroyed surely by death if not by the lovers themselves.

Why do You let this happen?

Your answer doubtless is that You can't stop it. That's the answer I'm getting all the time from You these days and I guess I have to accept it. Still, why do You permit us to have young love if it is to be taken away from us again?

Your answer, I suppose, is that it will be given back to us again, that indeed You are young love, that You love us like young lovers do and that young love is one of the best hints we have of what You are like.

I'm going to have to think that one over as the year ends.

December 31

Despite my resolution of only yesterday to swim and write this journal before the day begins and despite getting up an hour earlier this last day of the year, I find that I have only a few minutes before I must leave for SMW and the New Year's Eve Mass. I'm sorry. I wanted to at least honor my resolution to the extent of greeting

You this last day of the year and thanking You for all our gifts before I rush off. I'll try to be back. Protect me on the slippery streets.

January 1

HAPPY NEW YEAR!

It's a gray, grim day and I'm getting a late start because I was out late last night. So once again, on the first day of the year my resolution to begin the day with a swim and a prayer is half frustrated because the pool was already crowded at 10:30.

I'm trying, which is what I know I am expected to do.

I look at the calender for the two and a half weeks before I leave for Arizona and suddenly it seems jammed again. It makes me feel weary even before it begins.

I shouldn't be complaining on the first day of the year, a new beginning, a clean sweep, in the imagery of the popular media, and the end of the "holidays" and the real beginning of winter—despite the subzero weather we've already endured here in the middle west. I should be offering thanks for the blessings of the last year and asking for Your help and protection during 1990, one of the last years of my life by any reasonable actuarial reckoning.

So I am grateful for the last year and for the opportunities of the years to come. I want to be protected, should it please You to do so, (and why wouldn't it!) from ill-health, and anger, and cynicism, and disillusion, and weariness and discouragement. I think I've proved that I can bounce back from most of these troubles if given half a chance. I guess what I'd particularly want this year would be a somewhat less harried and hurried life, a lot less times when I leave my rooms in a mad rush because I have not left myself enough time.

I learned last year that the "flow" condition in which I work is a blessing. But like most other blessings in the human condition it is not an unmixed blessing. It can become so compelling, so exhilarating as to be almost an addiction, an obsession not so much with work as such but with the rewards, the high I suppose, that the process of creation bestows. The exhilaration is not wrong, quite the contrary it is a grace in itself (for which many thanks) but I need to temper it with more time for relaxation and reflection, times which to be honest often seem empty because the exhilaration is gone. Maybe in Tucson, when I finally get there this month, I'll be able finally to have a real vacation. Please help me to do so. I really need to prove to myself that I'm still capable of a vacation.

January 2

DURING Carol's funeral on Saturday I did a lot of thinking about You (and I must express my gratitude that on the slippery street I did no more than bump a fender against an abutment). There is no way the existence of a reflective creature like us can be explained by chance. Someone has to be responsible for thrusting us into existence. For the moment that someone seems unable to protect us from suffering and death. Fair enough, though there is much mystery here. In the long run, we believe that the someone in question will wipe away all our tears.

Is that belief justified? I argue this morning (at 6:00 AM, as You well know) that the fact of our existence justifies that belief. No one but a monster would have thrust us into existence knowing that our self-conscious lust for life would be frustrated, knowing that we would develop a conviction, however tentative, that we were loved if that conviction were false. So either You're a monster or a lover.

Fair enough argument? Where is it wrong? Either love or monstrous evil (uncaring, unreasoning) must be responsible for the universe and for us. If love, then all that we do and are survives. If not, then we are victims of a cruel joke. But can cruelty produce the love we see all around us? I rather think not.

I'm sorry for going through this rather logical and syllogistic argument on an early morning of the new year, but it seems that it is the nature of our human nature that periodically we must reflect this way (like every day!) to make sure of the ground on which we stand. I do intend to continue with my reflection on You as young love, a shattering insight if I've ever had one (and delightful too), beginning tomorrow, but I thought it right that first I get this much less poetic observation on the record.

January 3

THE notion that You are not only love but young love has been flitting around in my head for the last several days. If I wasn't so absorbed by this book on fidelity I would write a poem about it. I'll do that next week or when I get to Tucson. For now I will begin to reflect on this metaphor.

Everyone admires young love. When a couple announces their engagement and their plans for marriage, they are thought to be wonderful in their happiness and confidence in the future. We all know that it isn't going to be easy for them and that the first blush of young love will disappear quickly—by the end of the second year of marriage according to the data I'm working with. Yet we think that young love is glorious if transient and we hope that the thrill of romance will recur at least intermittently in their lives.

My data suggest that this scenario may be inaccurate and that about a sixth of married men and women are able to sustain such enthusiasm through their marriage. Young love may be tougher and more durable than the folk wisdom would have us believe.

The young lover (at whatever age) sees the spouse through eyes of love. The lover is a paragon of all perfections, kind, gentle, exciting, mysterious, romantic, etc. Is young love blind or does it see what is really in the lover, albeit latently, and excite, however temporarily, the lover's real self?

Sometimes one, sometimes the other I suppose.

Young love can be crazy, confident, consoling, daffy, delirious, delightful, dangerous, deceptive, exciting, exhilarating, ecstatic, foolish, frivolous, fanatical, grand, glorious, gripping, hilarious, heedless, heavenly, indulgent, idiotic, insightful, jolly, joyous, jubilant, kinky, killing, liberating, mad, maudlin, moody, nice, nutty, outlandish . . . but enough of the alphabet. Love, as they say in Brazil, is eternal but it does not last.

That proverb summarizes the conventional wisdom about love. It does not, however, seem to fit my data. More to the point here, however, it does not seem to fit You, You who may be and indeed claim to be young love personified.

Is that not the metaphor or the sacrament of the Song, not merely that You are Love but Young Love with all the delight and the craziness of the young lover. You are, if one is to believe the sources behind which You lurk, as madly in love, as heedlessly in love as the worst—or the best—of the young lovers.

Do I dare apply all those adjectives that I spun together—and which are a poem in the making—to You? It doesn't seem right even though You have legitimated it, indeed insisted upon it.

Do You have a teenage crush on me, like the lovers have on each other in the song?

That's a tough metaphor. I'll be back to it.

In the interim, however, the only answer to the question is yes.

January 4

I THINK the reason that young love is so frightening is that one can never be sure that it will last, not after the first time anyway. One learns to hedge one's bet in love relationships, though romance always seems eternal even if in the back of our heads we know enough to be suspicious.

It's wonderful when it's going on, but the let-down, we are dimly aware, will be terrible when it finally comes. Young love is too good to be true.

Is that what we hold against You? Will You be like all the other young lovers in our life? Will You disappear? Or will our relationship with You settle down to a routine without excitement and without romance?

There are times, with all respect, when that seems to be the case, when You flit away just as does the flighty young lover, times when You, again You should excuse the expression, seem as shallow as a teenager.

That's mystery, I suppose. Or maybe it's in the nature of human nature that we can't be open all the time to the demands of romantic love that You make on us. It is a burden to be loved intensely by someone else, a delight but also a time-consuming responsibility. Your romantic love for me imposes on me tremendous demands for response. Life is crowded enough as it is.

I suspect that one of the reasons human lovers permit their response to romantic love to fade is weariness. It is impossible to live at the peak all the time. Even radicals, it was once said, have to sleep. So, too, do lovers, at times not in each other's arms.

If a human lover can be an extra burden because of the demands that the lover makes, what about You?

I don't think weariness is the only reason why it's hard to picture You as a young lover. It's part of the explanation, however. More important, as I propose to reflect tomorrow, is the fact that romantic love is frightening. Demanding and frightening.

January 5

WHY is it frightening to be loved by a determined romantic lover?

Because the lover might take away all of You? That's what young love wants—everything. Such a demand might take away the control a person has on life. No, it will certainly deprive one of that control. Life will become a roller coaster, exhilarating ups and depressing downs, moments of ecstasy and moments of agony. Romantic love deprives one of a stable, orderly, routine life.

No one likes that prospect. I certainly don't. I resent interruptions when I'm at work—terribly these last few days as I'm sure You've noticed. The demands of a romantic lover guarantee interruptions all the time. The lover wants Your life, wants to remove control from You and take possession of it. In the hands of a romantic lover You don't know what's going to happen next—or when it's going to happen. Roller coasters are OK for brief interludes, though as You may well remember the only time I ever got on one I was sick for three days (it was an exciting event, I'll admit that, but You equipped me with a defective inner ear). Who would want to live on one?

The advantage in a human romantic lover over a divine one is that the former has to eat and sleep and can't be making demands, did I say silly demands, on You all the time. A divine romantic love is capable of perpetual and eternal silliness.

Did I say that about You?

Well?

You didn't deny it did You?

Last spring, influenced by George Coyne and the Jesuits at the Speculo Vaticano, I accused You of being a teenage God; now I'm suggesting that You're a teenage God with a romantic crush on me (and everyone else too, but that's their problem).

Is that unfair? Or, like all metaphors about You, does it err by defect rather than excess?

Sure, You have more sense than a teenager with a crush. But do You really? If You do, how come You got involved with us?

Love is never sensible, is it?

January 6

SOMEHOW I didn't get to this Epiphany entry until the end of the day—thus for my New Year resolutions. I was busy getting ready for my annual Twelfth Night party, which was very nice and for which thanks. I wonder at the end of parties like this why we bother with parties, which is a terribly uncatholic and unchristian thing to think and is doubtless the sign of how tired I am. I'd better go to bed now.

January 7

I'M still running. These are crowded, busy days with parties and obligations wherever I turn. No time. It was naive of me to think there would be time.

I hope it will be better tomorrow, but I must leave for

New York and the Today Show. I'll try to say something while I'm on the way.

I know You wouldn't want me to miss anything that I have to do today.

January 8

THE worst thing about the whole Christmas season is taking down the tree and the crib and the lights and the decoration. I did that yesterday on the run. Now all the color and brightness of Christmas has been stowed away for another year. Even the Christmas music is back in the boxes where the tapes and discs belong.

Sad business. I did stick it out till Twelfth Night. These days most folks take down the tree after New Years, in a hurry to end Christmas. I'd like to prolong it till the 13th, the octave of Epiphany, but we don't have octaves anymore.

There is a particularly sad aspect of it when one gets older. Will I be here next Christmas to take the decorations out and put them up again? At best I have only a few Christmases left. Each one is precious and I hate to see one of them pass by.

'Cuse the interruption.

Anyway I was feeling sorry for myself because of the end of Christmas, forgetting that in the world to come every day is Christmas and that even in this world every day is potentially Christmas as long as there is joy in one's heart. Life goes on, the river can't be slowed down. There will always be Christmas anyway.

January 9

HOME from New York. Dead tired.

January 10

AS I glance over the last couple of days I realize how badly this journal of prayers has deteriorated. The social demands of Christmas and leaving here for Tucson have filled up every day and every night. I'm tired from running, from responding to demands, from rushing all the time.

I know You love me even when I'm on this treadmill. I know moreover that there's not much I can do about this treadmill. Most of the demands are legitimate or legitimate enough.

I'm also fed up with rising at 5:00 every morning to get my work done or at least make progress on it before the phone starts to ring. I used to do that when I was writing. Now I do it almost all the time.

Maybe it will be better when I get to Tucson. I sure hope so.

Back in December I was congratulating myself on how well I felt despite the work of the semester. Now, with no other major work (well, except the fidelity book) I am exhausted by running around. I grow angry even when I think about the demands.

I'm kind of in a bad mood this morning, You say?

Sure am. And it's not just the trip back and forth to New York.

Today is the last day I get up at 5:00. Absolutely and regardless of what has to be done tomorrow.

I know You love me even when I'm grouchy. I know even that there's no point in having a Lover unless You can complain periodically. I know finally that You can't do anything about my complaints.

January 11

I'M much better today, partly because the sun is shining brightly and partly because I've about caught up with the work for my pre-Tucson transition. I guess my frantic rush to do the fidelity book is responsible for much of the pressure on me, not directly but indirectly because a lot of other things got compressed into the last week.

I am persuaded that it is all right to work that way for a week or two or three, but no longer. That's why I hope that Tucson this year will be a real vacation. Help me to make it so.

Now to the matter of You as Young Love. I put together quite hastily yesterday my Saint Valentine's edition of the *Mail Box Parish*, lifting, as You well know, since You know everything before I ask, a number of passages from this journal. I haven't written the poem yet, but I promise I will get to it over the weekend.

I was struck by how outrageous the metaphor is. It slips as all metaphors do because young love is often ephemeral, nothing more than passing infatuation, intense without depth. But the young love that is renewed on Valentine's Day is not passing because it has endured in marriage. The young love I have discovered in my study of marriage is not transient either. The romance of older people, one for another is hardly an infatuation. So You as Young Love are eternal young love, young love without the transiency—a crush, if I may, which never ends.

You have a crush on me! That's what the metaphor means. An eternal crush.

No way to get away from that if the sources are to be believed.

Wow!

I've been loved in many different ways in my life, some of them undoubtedly could be called crushes. Usually they were scary, sometimes attractive, sometimes not. In Your case, You are patently very attractive and very scary.

I'm going to have to cope with the metaphor in poetry. In prose it is too much.

Altogether.

January 12

ONE of the things I'm going to do when I get to Tucson a week from today is read through this journal and see if I can make any sense out of the one who wrote it.

I want to do the poem today, at least start it. I'll be back with it later on.

God (You) willing.

January 14

FORGIVE ME. No poem yet. The beginning of metaphors for the metaphor lurk in my imagination, but there was too much again today, made worse by the scratch on my eye from the contact lens this morning. I'm a basket case to tell the truth, not operating on all cylinders and yet trying to do a lot of things. This will be a crazy week. Help me through it and make me rest in Tucson.

I had supper with Erika tonight. She is very worried about David who probably won't last much longer. So much pain, so much suffering. I must call him before I leave for Tucson—on Thursday. He and Joan are so gallant. Would I be that gallant under the pressure of pain and ebbing life?

I'll die any way You want me to die, not that I have a choice in the matter. Help me to do it when my time comes as a faithful lover of Yours with total confidence in Your love, no matter what happens. What good is faith if it does not see one through tragedy and suffering—of which I have had on balance not all that much in my life, and practically none of it physical. I'm going to bed now. I'll try my best to get some of that poem down by tomorrow morning.

I love You, even when I'm so tired I can hardly think anymore.

January 15

ONLY a few more days before Tucson. I can hardly wait.

I was thinking yesterday as I was dashing around whether it is possible to integrate the metaphor of You as young love with the suffering, terrible suffering, that exists in this world.

Andrew Greeley

If young love is a scary roller coaster ride, might the suffering be the plunge downward on the ride? Might it be that after it's all over we'll see suffering as nothing more than that? Might the love which is at the center of everything be so powerful and so rewarding that the worst suffering of this life does not seem like anything worse than a downturn on the bobbs or some similar amusement park terror?

Can I say this about the holocaust? About the unnecessary death of a child? About the suffering of someone I love?

It is not a notion with which I feel all that easy and certainly not one I would want to preach in quite that form. Yet has not Your son told us that eye has not seen nor ear heard nor has it entered in our hearts what You have prepared for those who love You? While the rhetoric of the matter may be open to debate, the factuality does not seem to be. Our sufferings, so horrendous now, will be seen as minor in the consummation of Your romantic love for us.

Is that not pie in the sky?

Well, it often has been an excuse for not responding to the problems of this world. But it need not be. And it applies especially to those human sufferings for which there are no answers, like, most terribly of all, death. The promise of love to come does not make death any less painful. It only makes the pain more tolerable because it says that however terrible the pain it will soon be overwhelmed by love.

That's the promise. I see no more problem in believing in it than believing in You. Why stop at half a loaf? A God who is any God at all would do just what You

say You will do. A God who would do less is not worth
having as a God.

Mystery, mystery.

January 17

ONE of the interesting metaphors which I heard the
night before last (one among many) at my supper with
Wall and Shea was Jack's notion that we are born into
a second womb—that is the world in which we live is
a womb from which we are born at the time of death
into another world. We emerge from one womb into another and at the end of our life emerge from the second
womb, painfully as at the time of birth.

Therefore we live now in a womb, in a "pre-natal"
stage of development. We are struggling to be born.

That's marvelous poetry—it makes You a mother giving birth to us at least several times and maybe indefinitely. (That gives me an idea for another poem. Maybe
when I get to Tucson I'll do a "God cycle").There is no
reason to believe that the womb of this cosmos out of
which we are born at the time of death is the last of
wombs. Maybe we stay in our pre-natal condition for
a long time, going through many births.

That sounds a bit like John Hicks' theology. I don't insist on it for the moment (not that my insistence does
much good in a conversation with You!). The point is
that the "death is birth" metaphor can be developed and
enriched.

Is it true? Am I really caught up in an ongoing birth
process. Is life really "pre-natal?"

Andrew Greeley

If I believe You, then of course it's true. It's a long hard birth but it is nonetheless birth. Death is the beginning not the end. Enter again Blaise Pascal, about whom I talked last night at the seminar. Gambling on You makes sense, it's a fair wager, an insurance investment.

More than that, however, it is a leap of love. I believe that I am passing through a womb towards further birth.

January 18

ONE more day and them I'm out of here to Tucson. It's not so much the weather that I crave, because it's not cold here now, but the peace of getting away from the demands here. I must not let the demands increase out of control in Tucson.

I had a nice letter from Jack Coons about Your vulnerability. He writes: "Whatever makes us free must, by definition, be vulnerable to rejection by the liberated agent. So if God's primary will is to free man (note, he means humankind, doesn't he?) his other will—for community—is subordinate and might better be called hope. Having chosen to be vulernable in hope, God remains impregnable in will."

Elegantly stated, huh? God hopes for community with us. You hope that we will respond but Your will for our freedom is impregnable: You won't cheat to create community with us at the price of taking away our freedom.

Elegant and scary. Another metaphor for You—a God who hopes, a teenage, vulnerable, hoping God caught up in a young romance love affair.

Truly when I get settled in Tucson I will work on this

God cycle of poems which currently run around my head. They will be relaxing and good prayer, both of which I desperately need at the time.

I'll be back tomorrow morning before I finish my packing for Tucson. I am so tired right now.

January 19

IN three hours I'll be on the plane to Tucson where the weather alas is apparently terrible.

I have two introductions to write and an article to revise and that's all. I hope to do the God poems which are rushing around in my head and nothing else for at least a month. Help me to keep that resolution. I will read, watch videotapes, go to films, reflect and relax.

Or so I intend.

Even thinking about that raises some of the burden of tension. Shea said the other night that faith includes the confidence that the world is basically supportive, that we have the internal and external resources to cope with tragedy and suffering. This is an extraordinary statement, but it also seems to be, on reflection, nothing more than a description of human nature. Our ability to respond with grace is not irresistible, but it's there just the same. As I used to say in the seminary, they can scare You with an exam only once. Then You discover that after it's over You're still alive and life goes on. So with my surgery a couple of years ago and the settlement of the suit. You survive and life goes on.

Is it that way at the end of life? Is the consistent experience of life merely a genetic adaptation of a reflecting creature or is it a hint of explanation? Or, and I know that this is what You're going to whisper in my ear, both, both adaptation and sacrament?

Naturally it's the last: the benignity of the universe, even in the face of malace or blind evil, is a hint of Your envelope (*umwelt* Your German friends say) of love.

I do trust that envelope, though sometimes my frantic activity, especially like the last couple of weeks, suggests that I don't. Part of me doesn't, part of me does, and much of me loves the activity, which is fine, and loves it too much, which is not fine at all.

Well, with Your help the activity will slow for the next month.

I love You. Take care of me during the trip.

January 20

IN Tucson and organized. And feeling very old for some reason.

Maybe because I am old.

It's the end of the day and I'm tired. More tomorrow.

January 21

IT'S warming up here in Tucson and the sky is blue and I'm beginning to relax, though I did break my promise about no work: I woke up this morning with another idea for the fidelity book (which You undoubtedly planted in my head overnight). It was sufficiently important that I dispensed myself from my promise—on the pretext that

You would want me to do the chapter—and did the analysis. After I'm finished with it later on today, I'll revoke the dispensation.

I'm kidding as You well know about dispensations. I decided that it ought to be done. No more.

I've said that before? Well, yes.

But an idea like the one this morning was an inspiration of the Spirit! Wasn't it?

Anyway, I don't feel so old any more. A week of swimming and sitting in the warmth and reading and reflecting will make a new person out of me. It took two days, as it always does, to get organized here. Now I'm ready for the good part of the trip.

It will also be necessary, as I work on these God sonnets, to think about death, my death which cannot be all that far away as time goes. I don't want to be morbid but I do want to be sensible. Shea's point about releasing Yourself into the embrace of the world is surely well taken. Those who die peacefully have already done that. Or perhaps more precisely, they have accepted the natural process and the help that process gives them, help which You have built into our evolution and into the world. Do not go gentle into that good night? Well, yes and no. It's all right to protest against the failing of the light, so long as You know it has to fail and that protest and surrender are not incompatible.

They only become so when one loses trust in what Nozick calls one's most basic experiences and what I call You. I can protest against the fact of dying and still accept whatever it brings.

Help me to understand that truth and throw my trust utterly into Your hands.

Andrew Greeley

January 22

RAIN in Tucson today. Ugh.

I encountered three different metaphors for You in today's reading. The psalmist depicts You as one who grants victory, military victory in this case I think. Saint Matthew tells the family story of the crazy farmer. Louise Erdrich in the poems I am now reading imagines You as a furious and dangerous lover from whom it is necessary to hide. It reminds me of her timberwolf image from our correspondence.

Here I am thinking of You as a daffy teenager, a vulnerable lover, and young love!

Who is the romantic?

Obviously all the metaphors tell us something about You, that's what metaphors are supposed to do. The crazy farmer, not unlike my daffy teenager, is perhaps no less fiercely determined than the timberwolf. While You are vulnerable because You have given us freedom there is a fierce demanding warrior-like passion in Your vulnerability.

I am trying to combine metaphors into theology, a legitimate enough activity, God (You) knows. But besides the point in metaphor creation. It is of the nature of the metaphor and the story contained in it that it need not be harmonized with other metaphors, but it can be permitted to stand on its own to excite wonder and awe.

Some appeal to one person, some to others. I don't resonate much to Louise's fear of You. Maybe I ought to. Maybe there is too much tenderness in my groping attempts to be in touch with You and not enough reverential awe. I am, after all, trying to communicate with the one who created the Big Bang, and arguably billions of Big Bangs, maybe more reverential awe, more holy terror would be appropriate.

Yet I have to take as definitive the parables of Jesus and today the story of the crazy farmer, so soft on his workers that he needed medical help. The cause of the Big Bang as crazy with love!

Anyway and for the record, I acknowledge the Big Bang (about which the NYT debated yesterday) and the unimaginable power behind it. I am scared stiff of You and with reason.

But that only makes me love You all the more.

January 23

IT'S nine o'clock at night. Despite my good intentions to be work on this journal in the early part of the day, I am here at the end. I still haven't quite routinized my life here to think about what must be done after I wake up.

Anyway, the delay gives me the opportunity to thank You for the wonderful weather—70 and sunny. I actually sat in a poolside lounge and read, something I haven't done in a long, long time. A few more days like this and I'll feel like a new person!

I read part of a book of short short stories, some of which are brilliant. I think I'll try my hand at those again. One of them was by Margaret Atwood, who is not my favorite writer. It was kind of a tussle with the form itself, arguing that the form seemed to demand a happy ending no matter what happened to the various people in it in the course of the story. To illustrate this she made the story a series of endings, all of which were the same, no matter what happened. Then she said all the endings were false because in the end everyone would die anyway.

The question, she concluded, is not when but why.

It's the same question Louise Erdrich struggles with in her poetry, she with far more a sense of Your presence than Atwood possesses. Louise knows You're there, she's not sure that she likes You very much, though she does admit today that You are probably weary of our non-response.

The problem Atwood contends with is that stories tend to give meaning, even if the meaning is negative. Indeed even an unhappy ending is in effect a meaning. But what if You are a storyteller who doesn't believe in meaning at all?

It's a tough position to be in, especially when You face up to the death question which lurks in every story. We all know that the happy ending is only finite, that the lovers enjoy their happiness only for a time. The story gives us a hint of hope that it might not be so, that love does not die, that it is at least as strong as death.

Louise's exact quote which I now add the next day reads (St. Clare talking about weary parent birds feeding their offspring): "For the parents were weary as God is weary./We have the least mercy on the one/ who created us/ who introduced us to this hunger."

I talked to my friend Marilyn on the phone tonight, caught her in a burst of tears because a friend's mother had died. "I can't cope with death," she said. Who can?

Perhaps Louise is right. You must grow weary of our doubts. You could take the position I have always maintained that You've given us every possible sign of Your love that You could and still left us free. We don't look at the signs.

Weary with us You may be, but You still love us and that's what counts.

And I love You, however late and however imperfectly.

January 23

I'M back on my morning schedule again—and feeling happy too that most of my excess Christmas weight has been shed. The Church should adapt to the times and have the real Lent right after January 1, don't You think?

I've been rereading *The Edge of Sadness* by Edwin O'Connor in preparation for writing an intro to the Thomas More edition. There was an edge of sadness about reading it. When I first read the book almost thirty years ago I was twenty years younger than Father Hugh Kennedy, who is really the protagonist as well as the narrator (like Kevin Brennan); now I'm seven years older. Moreover the bishop in the book still reminds me of the late Cardinal Meyer (and he is a German from Milwaukee!) who died much too soon. Finally the picture of the priesthood in the book is accurate for the time.

You know that I am no fan of clerical culture. I despise the deliberately cultivated incompetence and mediocrity, the rigid and punitive envy, the insensitive arrogance which can be characteristic of the priesthood—all cultivated during our seminary education.

Yet the relationship between priest and people, the exchange of care and loyalty, the authentic reverence, the dedication and generosity were rich resources which we have wasted. Curiously enough, as I have often written, we are more important to them as religious leaders now than we were then but we can't—or don't want to—see it. They tolerate so much slovenly incompetence because they still look forward, forever optimistic, to the day when the good priest comes to their parish.

Lots of luck!

Well, there's no point in being nostalgic. My fictional Father Laurence O'Toole McAuliffe is the same age as Hugh Kennedy, but post-conciliar rather than pre-conciliar and manic-depressive rather than merely depressive. But the faith and the dedication are still there. The priesthood has survived a long time and will survive the present idiocy. Moreover the religious leadership, which is at the essence of the priesthood will survive too, not because we want it to but because the laity won't give it up.

Thank You for calling me to the priesthood.

January 25

In her poem I read this morning—the one on Holy Orders—Louise speaks of the thin, dry noise a leaf makes scratching against a leaf. I'm not sure exactly what she means by that, but I think the poem can be read as the cry of a discouraged priest. I'm not quite that discouraged now, not on the surface of my personality anyway. I know the feeling, however of having the impact of a leaf scratching on a leaf.

I do a lot of talking, in my columns, in my fiction, in my nonfiction, on TV, and all of it put together is little more than a leaf scratching against a leaf from the point of view of affecting people or from the point of view of eternity.

I do it because You do what You can do and what You must do and because with Your help it has some minor impact. But it's not all that important. When I am gone, the Church and the world will go on pretty much the same as it always has.

This is not pessimism or despair (actually, I feel fine at the end of this first week in Tucson) but realism. You're far more important than my work to my life, to say nothing of the rest of Your creation. That does not mean that I stop trying. It means rather that I ought to see my own efforts in the context of cosmos and eternity (what a nifty title for a book that would make!). I have a role to play and if I don't play what I am supposed to do in life does not get done. Therefore I work—and to the extent that it is possible enjoy my work. But I also realize that for all my words I am still a leaf scratching against a leaf.

January 26

END of the first week in Tucson and I already feel rested and relaxed, for which many thanks. I begin work on the sonnets next week.

Yesterday at the grocery (excuse me, I date myself),

at the supermarket, I bought a copy of *Life*'s "Best Photos of the 1980s." When I began to look through it, I realized that it was obscene. It didn't have any pictures of naked women, a minor obscenity compared to the way it intruded into death and dying. I don't want to reflect particularly on the immorality of the magazine, it's exploitation of death for our titilation (it enables the viewer to distance himself/herself from death and does not compell any thought about our own death) is not the subject about which I reflect this morning. Rather I ponder the terrible things that You permit to happen to Your sons and daughters in this world.

The most terrible picture is that of a little girl dying in a South American mudslide, her head and part of her chest above ground. The photographer says that there was nothing anyone could do and that the child was dying with dignity and bravery. Maybe there was nothing he could do, but to photograph that scene was a terrible obscenity.

But I don't blame him as much as I blame You. The kid was eminently lovable. Her parents loved her. I loved her, looking at her picture. You must have loved her too. You let her die horribly. How come?

The answer I knew well even before I began to write these words: You suffered more with her dying and her death than anyone else did, even more than she did. Your heart was wrenched with aching love more than mine was when I looked at the picture, far more. You suffer whenever one of us suffers, even more than we do.

I don't know what to make of that answer this Saturday morning in Tucson. I know that it's the only one I have. I know that I must go through it repeatedly in my life to reenforce it's power in my spirit. I know that how-ever incredible it may seem, it's the only one that holds back chaos, that puts meaning in the absurdity of life.

Again I reflect on Your terrible vulnerability. I don't want to add to Your hurt by seeming critical. As You well know, it's a question I must often ask. I don't under-stand Your powerlessness, short-run powerlessness I hastily add, in the face of the suffering of Your sons and daughters. I know only that if You are vulnerable, and I believe that You are, You must be weeping all the time.

I wish I could make Your pain go away.

January 27

IN the gospel passage this Sunday morning Jesus tells the parable of the wedding feast. There are a lot of dif-ferent interpretations, including the one that Matthew imposes on the story, which is obviously appropriate for the time of his gospel but neither for ours nor for the time of Your Son. However, the obvious theme, even if we can't quite get back to the original text, is that Jesus came to invite us to a party, to offer the kind of invita-tion that no one in their right mind would turn down—an irresistible invitation to a celebration.

Yet we manage to resist the invitation and not to cele-brate nor look like celebrants. I had a party for my sister at El Charro last night to honor her visit to Tucson to lecture at the University. It was a great party, good food, nice atmosphere, delightful guests (and I'm sure You were there enjoying it too). If I am to believe Jesus, that's what heaven will be like. Moreover that's what life on earth should be like for those who believe in Your love as He revealed it. Obviously there is tragedy and death as I reflected yesterday; but for a follower of Jesus the celebration is stronger than the wake (and those Irish who follow him, weirdly turn the wakes into celebrations).

For me now that means there must be joy in my life, I must live like a celebrant. From sour-faced saints, deliver us, O Lord, in the words of Teresa of Avila. I don't think I've ever been a sour-faced person, but only two weeks ago I was pretty worn out and testy. It has taken only a week here in Tucson and not an utterly relaxed week, either, to make me feel joyous again.

To feel like a celebrant in the middle of winter with the sun shining brightly and the temperature touching seventy doesn't require much effort. The trick would be to act like a person of joy and faith under other circumstances.

The best I can say about myself is that I have a lot of room for improvement.

I am a celebrant at a wedding feast not only at the Eucharist but every day and every moment of my life.

And You, my dear one, are the bride who has given Herself to me.

That sounds almost like blasphemy and I wouldn't dare say it unless it were clear from the data that You want me to say it.

Even then it sounds strange when I do.

January 28

I'M sure that You have arranged to produce, through the evolutionary process, a species which can't help hope. If hope is often hard to come by, it's even harder to get rid of when You don't want to hope. What else besides hope could keep men and women going in the midst of all the disasters of life. Hope is, as George Coyne said the other night, the human response to our astonishment that we're here at all.

On the level of ideas I'm sure that's why the species has always postulated You, not as the result of formal philosophical reasoning, though that points in the same direction too. If we are here, people say, then someone or Someone must be responsible.

That quick leap of understanding coexists with and is reenforced and reenforces our experience of You, our sense that we live in a broad and gracious envelope. That it is a crazy-in-love envelope and vulnerable one we needed Jesus to comprehend, but that too seems to fit the pattern, even if it is a dazzling revelation.

I encounter You in those little moments of "ordinary" love which explode when I meet friends out here that I haven't seen in months, an overflowing of goodness and giftedness which I take for granted and yet revere almost as magic. These friends didn't have to be here, but they are. In the surge of excitement at seeing them again I encounter grace and thus Grace. A world in which such events happen must be a world in which something wonderful or Someone Wonderful lurks.

That's not a philosophical argument, though one could

develop an argument from such an experience. It is an immediate, transient, and numinous encounter with g(G)race. You're there. Loving it, I'm sure.

One of our problems, certainly one of my problems, is that I am not sensitive enough to these minor miracles, these quick outbursts of grace, these brief interludes of grace, these soft rumors of angels which ought to tell me that You're near me, loving me all the time.

January 29

MY sister gave her talk at the U last night and was very well received which she richly deserved. Haiko Oberman, whom I often call the "last Protestant," was especially favorable in his comments. I couldn't help but think about what a distinguished career as a theologian she would have if she wasn't burdened by being my sister.

She used the metaphor of God as housewife in her presentation, God the caretaker who keeps the universe in order and centers creation in familial love. I had forgotten about that one, a brave image at a time when housewives are in ill repute (although my data show they are the happiest people in America). Yet the picture of You as the one who tends to the needs of the whole family of creation, each creature of which is protected with loving care is another startling yet valid one. I'll have to include that in my God sonnets which I hope to start working on this afternoon.

The lecture hall was filled for her talk last night, proof that religion still is popular, still has a hold on the minds and hearts of the young.

January 31

I FINALLY did the two poems yesterday. It's interesting how the piles of images and words which jam the preconscious finally come tumbling out when I give them a chance.

God The Romantic Lover

"Love is forever but it does not last."
— Brazilian parable
Paralyzed in a fragrant languid bog,
A victim of an incurable obsession,
Enveloped in a gentle rosy fog
A willing victim of sweet infection
I become a clown, a shameless naked slave,
Bounced between ecstasy and dejection
A lunatic on a roller coaster wave,
A fool, innocent of all discretion.

"God is love"—this is what it really means?
Is God that heedless of my imperfection?
Captivated by daffy romantic dreams?
God broken hearted by my rejection?
Lord of all creation only seventeen?
Does God dream love's death ends in resurrection?

God the Homemaker

She who makes my home, a habitat creates
Of concern amidst anonymity,

Andrew Greeley

A center which affection animates
And order, love and magnanimity.
At home my soul and body she repairs—
Broken heart, running nose, and bloody knee.
She dispenses healing and restoring care
Not to an insensate number but to me.

The universe is not cold and dry
An absurd, infertile singularity
Beneath an empty loveless darkened dome.
God hovers over it with a lullaby,
And, bathing the cosmos with sweet charity,
She makes of it for each of us a home.

Do I believe both these metaphors I ask myself (as I promise I will continue to refine and rework the images)?

I find them both enormously appealing. They represent the mystical element in my personality, insofar as there is one! They are the pictures of Who I think You Are. Moreover You have given me grounds for believing that You're like these images, so if I'm wrong it's Your fault.

The problem is the other way, isn't it? If I accept these metaphors of You as a young lover and a homemaker, why don't I live that way? Or live that way more of the time? If these images crowd into my preconscious, why don't they animate my life?

The answer I guess is that my faith isn't strong enough. Make it stronger.

February 1

THIS morning I read Psalm 49 and the final days passage in Saint Matthew. The metaphors are very different from my own. I continue to encounter this critique of my own homey, sentimental, and romantic images of You from the scriptures. Of course my images are based on other passages of the scriptures and the images of You as judge and Lord of Creation need to be critiqued by the images I like. All our metaphors fail by defect and by the fact that each one can at best respond only to one set of signals You send us.

My images are consoling and reassuring, terrifying only if You think an aroused romantic lover or a determined homemaker is terrifying—which of course she is. I think most people most of the time need to be reassured, need to be threatened by too much love instead of threatened by anger and judgment. Life is tough enough as it is, even in our comfortable modern America, without piling on them terror and guilt more than they already feel. Perhaps in an environment where Jesus' message of love was really taken seriously, where people wallowed in Your love, then the message of terror should be delivered more vigorously. Perhaps also to the modern Pharisees, those who are so confident that they have signed You up on their side (like some Church bureaucrats), need to be terrified. Most of us need, oh, so desperately, to be reassured so that we can take the risk of more gracious and generous living.

Yet my collection of sonnets, which already do indeed

acknowledge You as the Lord of creation, need to be corrected by today's images too.

As I reflect on that notion and try to picture a metaphor of You as judge incorporated into a poem, I end up not with the image of judge but of judge-who-is-a-lover. The love metaphor, once it is conceded and explored, becomes the "privileged" metaphor, one that takes over and dominates all the rest.

I am overwhelmed again, almost to the point of tears, by the picture of You as the vulnerable lover, fragile in the face of the freedom You have given us. That is an image which will always be dominant in my mind, even if it has yet to pervade my life the way it ought to.

I am sorry, so sorry for hurting the One I love.

February 2

THE feast of the purification and of Saint Brigid, my patron, feast of light, candlemass day. The candles blessed originally because the station procession in Rome started in the Forum before sunrise. Brigid the patron of spring and new life and poetry and story telling. We could use some light here in Tucson. The last three days have been dark and cold and rainy. This morning the mountains behind my house were dusted with snow. And it looks like the storm will follow me to Chicago on Sunday when I go home to celebrate my birthday.

As Sir George Solti said on his seventy-fifth birthday, the numbers are certainly high and cannot go too much higher. Most of my life is over. Most of my feasts of Saint

Brigid have already been celebrated. Most of my springs are behind me.

Yet I can hardly complain. It has been an exciting and happy life if not the one I would have designed for myself. As I often have said, there's no point in fighting the Holy Spirit because She's going to have Her way regardless. Since You are the Holy Spirit that applies to You, doesn't it?

February 3

I READ the Fiftieth Psalm this morning, an act of contrition. It's appropriate as I approach my birthday and review my life. I am sorry for all the things I have done wrong in my life. The notion of what is wrong has changed since I learned the catechism and even since I learned moral theology. Now I understand that You can keep all the rules and still lead a vain and sinful life and that You can break the rules and still be a good person, although the rules are still important and must be kept. Ideally one leads a good life in basic orientation AND keeps the rules. One does not lie, cheat, steal, kill, commit adultery, covet, envy, but that is not enough. One also must live openly and generously and lovingly.

I have not lied or cheated or robbed or killed or violated women. I have been angry many, many times, though usually within myself. I have stored up angers though to be fair to myself I have never rejected reconciliation. I have perhaps been too eager to fight.

By the standards of the books on which I was raised

Andrew Greeley

I have led a good life, though the books would surely not approve of my criticism of Church authority (in which the books would have been wrong since Church authority, like all authority, needs criticism). Moreover I have made use of my talents or at least some of my talents which was not in the books though it certainly is in the Bible.

None of this, I now know, is enough, not nearly enough. While as I've said yesterday I've been happy, I have not been joyous enough, confident enough, secure enough in Your love. Most of the mistakes I have made as a public person (a role I did not expect and for which I was unprepared) have come from that weakness and the propensity to cut myself off from those whom I perceived (often correctly) as betraying me. I did not take into account the impact I have on others, not believing in myself enough to realize this impact (until recent years anyway).

To be blunt, I have lived a life of action of the sort I think You approve. I have not lived a life of faith, or to be precise a life of nearly enough faith. I have not understood adequately the nature and power of Your love for me—that is the root cause of my failures great and small. I'm sorry, truly, truly sorry. I'll try to do better. I have, to put the same matter a little differently, been too busy with too many things and not busy enough with You. Again I'll try to do better.

I've let myself be worn out by too much action and not enough contemplation—it's as simple as that.

Moreover, as I said yesterday my mixture of vulnerability and outspokenness has also been a problem. There's no way I'm not going to be vulnerable. The criticism has never stopped me but I have permitted hurt to turn into anger and discouragement and that has dimmed my faith.

I'm not sure what to do about that exactly, except to resist the propensity as best I can.

Tomorrow I'm going to try to work up enough nerve to write about women, not so much an examination of conscience because I have not violated or exploited them but to review my relations with them to see where they need to be improved.

I know the answer already. Although I am gentle and sensitive with them I must be more gentle and sensitive. No man has ever erred by being too gentle with women.

February 4

I AM writing this on the plane flying to Chicago for a birthday party tonight. I would much rather stay in Tucson, but family and friends insist on the Chicago party so there isn't much choice.

Mind You, I'm not opposed to parties, but why the birthday has to be celebrated on the exact day escapes me. However, I am grateful that the folks who want to have this party love me enough to insist that, a) they have the party and b) that I fly home for it.

Would I be upset if they didn't insist? Sure, I never claimed to be consistent, did I?

I looked up life expectancy yesterday, not deliberately (or so I tell myself). I was leafing through the new Almanac searching for the height/weight tables for my family report and came upon life expectancy. Turns out that on the average I could last till I'm eighty-two—twenty more years. Of course no one is average, but there are long-lived as well as short-lived genes in the clan and my doctor claims the evidence indicates that I have the former.

Eighty-two is a nice age, especially if the body and the mind hold up. I would not want to be a vegetable but it would be interesting to see what this rapidly changing world looks like in 2012.

That's all up to You. I accept whatever plans You have for me. I could of course not make it back to Tucson tomorrow night. That's unlikely too, but it's all up to You, more or less. What I mean is that no matter what happens to me, You will turn it into good things in the long run, like the wonderful ending on the lips of the Polish priest at the end of *The Edge of Sadness*.

Those are perfect sentiments for a birthday eve.

Now about women. I suppose my propensities on that subject are clear enough from my novels. I like them, I enjoy them, I revel in their attention and love—as do all my male characters. They also like me, which is a constant surprise to me, something I never expected.

Obviously, I have created You in the image and likeness of the women I have most adored, so it's clear from these reflections how I feel about them. More precisely, I know You especially through Your self-disclosure through them.

I think I am reasonably good at being gentle with them, which as I noted yesterday, is the most important thing men have to learn about women. I am not so good at the other side of the coin, being firm with them. All love,

I take it, indeed all interaction with others must be a mix of gentleness and firmness, as inconsistent a demand as You ever put in the human condition. The man/woman relationship is merely a special variety of that.

My inability to draw the line (which may not be the best possible metaphor) with women is part of my larger inability to draw the line on those who intervene in my life space beyond appropriate measure. I have a hard time finding the middle ground between biting my tongue and explosive anger, with the latter rare but terrible when it does happen. Being trained in the priest role aggravates this problem, but in my case it didn't cause it.

I wonder what would have happened if I did not have a celibate vocation. I would have to have learned in the intimacy of marriage how to deal with friction and conflict and not terminate the relationship (or destroy love) through repressed anger.

Since I almost certainly would have married someone like the woman characters in my novels, such a nuanced response between repression and fury would have been a constant problem. Perhaps a constant delight too.

Well, the various states of life have their own problems and their own rewards. Like I have been saying a lot lately, it does no good to fight the Holy Spirit. I do think I am more sensitive and responsive to women than most married men and I don't think I would be that if I weren't a priest.

Conclusion from this birthday eve reflection?

'Tis clear enough, You eejit: be more sensitive and responsive.

February 5

MY sixty-second birthday. For all the exciting and happy years of my life, for all the opportunities, for my family, my friends, for my faith, for my vocation to the priesthood, for my talents, for my health, for Your love, for all the loves in my life, for my successes, for my failures from which I have learned, for these and all the other blessings of the last sixty-two years, my deepest thanks.

I'm typing this on the plane flying back from Chicago to Tucson. It's 8:30 Tucson time and we're about an hour and a half out of the city. I'm pretty well exhausted from the trip and from the emotional excitement of the two days. The party last night was deeply moving. I no longer have to be persuaded of the love my family and friends feel for me. I don't quite understand the reasons for that love, but it's so patent as to be overwhelming. Odd, as I write those words I find myself thinking that I really don't deserve all the love which was showered on me last night. That's a crazy notion. No one deserves love (except maybe You). It's not earned (and even You don't earn it). Rather it's pure gift. Anyway, a lot of people have given love to me, Yourself included, and just now I am overcome by that fact—last night almost to the point of tears.

Today was also traumatic, a reconciliation with an old friend, and a good reconciliation—for which much gratitude to You that I pushed my principles of going the extra couple of miles a number of times. I hope You don't mind my saying that I'm kind of proud of myself for acting like a Christian, even though You deserve the credit for nudging me into it.

It will take a night's sleep, swimming tomorrow, and some further reflection to sort it all out. Right now all I can say is that the day is kind of typical of my life. Oh yes, I almost forgot the interview with *Time* on the study before I left for the airport.

You never promised a quiet life. I never wanted a quiet life. And it's never been dull. A romantic like me couldn't ask for anything more.

Thank You with all my heart and soul.

February 7

I'M sure it's weariness from two long plane flights in two days but I am discouraged and depressed again. There's no specific content to it, just general frustration with all the bad things that are happening.

Right now I feel so tired that I wonder if my two weeks out here were any more than a superficial cure for profound weariness. The trip to Phoenix today and to L.A. on the weekend are not likely to improve my disposition much. But then I'll have a blessed month.

February 8

I FEEL better today, much better. Can't beat a good night's sleep to improve the view of the world. What a creature I am of bodily cycles—jet lag, light and darkness, weariness and refreshment. More than most people as far as I can tell. It's the way I am, the way You made me and it can't be changed. My mistake, I think, has always been to pretend that I'm immune from this particular kind of creaturehood that comes with being me. I should take time off after a plane ride instead of trying to plunge into the world as though the trip didn't happen.

Sometimes that's not so easy. At least I've progressed enough to know when I'm in a weary mood and not (most of the time) do anything radical or desperate. If I'd understood that ten years ago I would have had much less trouble.

February 9

A FEW days late, I want to use this octave time of my birthday to thank You for my parents. It has been so long —1947, 1963—that I have almost forgotten who they were, although they are still very much alive in my dreams. It's hard for me to get a focus on them, especially because when I was in my most formative years they were suffering from the terrible disappointment of the great depression. Yet before that they were surely happy and in the years that remained to them after the depression they also seemed happy. They were also plagued at the end of their lives by bad health (which, Thank You, I have so far been spared).

Yet they were surely good to me, especially in that critical ingredient in the life of all children, affection and support. So much of what I am today, especially the mix of wit and refusal to compromise, is little more than a carbon copy of them.

And my Catholicism, quite independent of what pope, bishops, and priests do, is also an inheritance. As is my priestly vocation.

I cannot say that I have any regrets about love not returned, regrets that so many people seem to have. No one ever loves enough. I didn't love them enough. Yet I did love them, they did know that, they could not have complained that there was no response from me to them. That I did respond to love with love of my own is a fact for which I will always be grateful to You.

I'm sure my talent with words is mostly an inheritance and my readiness to use the talent instead of being afraid of it was almost entirely their gift to me.

Would they approve of me now. What would Your poor mother say if she were alive to read Your books, I am occasionally asked—usually by those who haven't themselves read the books.

Both of them would have approved if only because I had written them and would be proud of what I have done with my life. That my work has made me a square peg in the priesthood, though that is not what I expected or intended, would have not bothered them in the least. It may in fact bother me more than them.

It is so difficult to relate to parents as one adult to other adults. There wasn't much chance for that in my life. I don't know how it would have worked. Nonetheless it will be interesting in the world to come to get to know them again.

Anyway, thank You for those who gave me my life and

nurtured it and passed on to me my religious heritage. Grant that I may continue to live up to the ideals they taught me.

February 10

JUDAS and Judith in today's readings—both dealers in treachery, one in a bad cause, one in a good cause. I think today we might have a different reaction to Judith's accomplishments than they did in her day. Maybe not; if the government can indict those it entices into crime and use sexual love to trap Washington's mayor maybe it would be all right for the Servants of the Holy One to do the same thing.

Dear God, will we ever learn that for followers of the Lord Jesus there is no difference between Judith and Judas, those who lie for the good of the Church and those who betray the Church and its Founder.

It's easy for me to take this position I suppose. I have no responsibility for protecting the Church from scandal, financial mismanagement, and sexual corruption. If I were in the position of the leadership I might see things differently. I hope however that I would not be so blinded by responsibility as to forget the difference between good and evil, between truth and falsehood, between honor and dishonor.

My own responsibility is different. Because of a series of events, mostly accidental, I often represent the Catholic heritage in the mass media, either directly or indirectly. This coming week as I try to respond to questions about my study of marriage I will be interviewed not only as a sociologist but also as a priest. Usually I don't do badly at combining those roles before the camera, but there's always a terrible risk of confusing my own personal image with the image of the Church, to worry more about what the viewers and readers will think of me than what they will think of the heritage I represent.

It's hard to sort out self-seeking and other-seeking. Some of the former is legitimate but it's difficult to know where the line ought to be drawn, especially since mostly it operates on a preconscious level and also because a person who plays many different roles has to balance these roles fairly in a few brief moments of air time.

I write this reflection this morning to remind myself of who and what I am and what I represent. Help me always to be clear about those truths.

February 11

MY LOVE,

I read in the paper the other day that there is a controversy among astronomers about whether more money ought to be spent on radio searches through space for signs of other rational life—the assumption of the supporters being that other rational creatures would use radio waves. The majority of astronomers seemed to think that it was a waste of money. Maybe we're the only ones, said a spokesman for one side of the debate, the majority side it would seem.

Maybe, and there are no scientific reasons for insisting that there are other forms of rational life abroad in the cosmos. Whether it is statistically improbable or statistically probable depends on what kind of statistics one uses. Right now it is a theological problem. Did the creator (You, but I haven't introduced You into the equation yet) who produced such an incredible array of stuff in the cosmos decide to settle for only one form of rationality?

Put that way and despite conservative theologians it seems most unlikely that there are not myriad forms of rational life around and about—and thus Your servants the science fiction writers are on the side of the angels in a couple of different ways.

Moreover when one begins to reflect on who You are and how You behave it seems to be quite impossible that You didn't spew rationality about Your creation in the same way You produced an incredible array of beings in this blue planet of ours.

The cosmos, as one of the characters in the story on which I am working puts it, is more wonderful than we could possibly imagine.

I believe that partly because I know something about the cosmos from my reading—and it becomes more wonderful the more we know about it. But mostly because I know that You, the source of all wonders, are indeed Wonder-full. So like John Dunne the Mick (also known as Duns Scotus) I accept the argument—if something is possible, then it is.

The minor premise in that argument is that if You can do something, You will.

And with the changes in Eastern Europe and the release of Nelson Mandela, You seem again to be busy in our blue planet.

Help me never to lose my awareness of wonder.

February 12

NOONTIME in Los Angeles. The interview went well this morning and the *Times* article was good. So our research on fidelity has at least established a foothold in the popular consciousness.

How do I get into such controversial areas of research? Perhaps because I cannot resist the new and the unusual project, though You would think that a study of marriage which finds out that it works pretty well would not be all that controversial, would You?

Anyway, while I'm pretty good at the TV appearance game and while it's a good thing that some priest has an opportunity to play in the game, I don't much like it, mostly because of the travel and the hotels and the poor sleep at night. If I never did another one again, I would not be especially unhappy.

I do hope it helps sell the book because then I will be able to begin phase two of the project next week and finish the analysis and writing by the end of April when I go to Budapest.

Here I am complaining about Los Angeles and the Beverly Hills hotel and I'm planning to go to Budapest and Prague!

The sun is out now, clearing away the morning fog and it's quite lovely. I was reflecting as I came in last night—with the news of the oil spill off Huntington Beach on TV and in the papers that this setting—mountains, valleys, and oceans is one of the most beautiful places in the world and how the city of Los Angeles, an ugly, smog-drenched urban sprawl is one of the ugliest places in the world. Driving back this morning from the ABC studio to the hotel on Hollywood Boulevard and Sunset Boulevard, I had the same thought. Cities don't have to be ugly but this one sure is and in such a wondrous setting.

I thought that the ecologists were right about protecting the earth and its beauty from corruption. I've always felt that way. You made this world a paradise, a park, and we're busy turning it into a garbage dump. While the enthusiams of the environmentalists and their self-righteousness and simplisms turn me off, their fundamental goal is unarguable.

Lake Michigan may be more polluted today than it was a hundred years ago, but it doesn't have any cholera bacteria which is a great improvement. Some price has to be paid for progress, but not as much as we have paid. Can't the lake be free of both pollution and cholera?

The Catholic imagination should have a lot to say on this subject but characteristically we are merely repeating the cliches of others instead of offering our own insights. Maybe I should try something like that in whatever time You leave me.

Anyway, thanks for the beauty of this world which gives me a hint of how beautiful You are.

February 13

I'M writing this on the plane flying back to Tucson. In the airport at LAX I did an interview with Vatican Radio about Saint Valentine and my research. It was a more intelligent interview than the Home show experience. I guess the latter goes with the territory.

Well, it's over and the study is done and it is on the record and if he has any luck in selling the book the day after tomorrow (and, with respect, I hope You'll see that he has a little bit of luck) we can go to the next phase. I'll spend the next month in Tucson going nowhere.

Right now I'm tired and discouraged again. I know that comes from travel and that after a swim and night's sleep I'll feel fine.

St. Valentine's Day

A GRIM day for a day of love and indeed a grim week which is part of a grim winter that's only marginally better here than it is in Chicago. Surely I might enter a respectful protest.

Today I want to reflect on the difficulty of love. Even the romantic love which we celebrate today needs to be renewed precisely because it cannot be sustained indefinitely in the face of friction, tension, weariness, and similar staples of the human condition. If love were easy we would not need Saint Valentine.

All kinds of love are difficult, no kinds are easy—and that includes You, my fine, wonderful, adorable (literally) Valentine. You don't make it easy, You really don't.

Anyway, in the poem I read this morning the poet describes a battle between a mother and child in a supermarket—a busy, nervous mother and a whining little kid. It's a scene I've seen often. It always tears at me and obviously it tore at the poet too.

The mother's language and violence are terrible. The kid's pain is appalling. Yet they love each other because mother and child always love one another—though in varying ways and degrees.

I tell myself that one can never judge from observing such an interlude what the quality of the relationship is like. The mother may be under great strain. The kid might be in a deliberately obnoxious mood—that is hardly unknown behavior. The mother may well have regrets later on. Under ordinary circumstances the two may relate to each other very well.

Yet there are times when the tone of the conflict suggests that this is the normal state of things between mother and child. Then I worry what the kid's life will be like—and what the mother's life is like now.

There is a young woman who works at a drugstore near here, very young (not 20), very pretty, and very angry—hostile, unpleasant, nasty. No wedding ring. She has a kid in day care, a fact which she moans about constantly. She does not want the kid, pretty clearly. He is a burden to her life, probably the cause of her anger.

I think when I see her frown that one so young ought not to be so unhappy and so angry. What chance does she have? What chance does the child have?

Protect them, help them, care for them, please. You love them both I know. You want them to love one another. Yet there are so many obstacles in the way of their love. As there are in the way of all love, including, heaven save me, my love for You.

On this Valentine's Day, help all lovers, which means all of us.

February 15

ALWAYS is not a very good film. It is too long, falsely sentimental, pseudo-religious. Moreover, Holly Hunter and Richard Dreyfus are two of my least favorite screen personalities. Their mannered acting is so self-conscious and so phony that I feel sick in my stomach especially when both of them are on the same screen.

Yet it was worth the effort to stay and see it as the third part of my escape from Tucson snow to a triple feature (first time since 1942!) for one reason: Steven Spielberg's marvelous decision to have Audrew Hepburn play You. Or Your Spirit which is the same as You.

Maybe it's the fact that I have grown old at the same time that this beautiful woman has grown old and that her face and smile now suggests mother rather than spouse. Anyway, her wise and tender love for the poor idiot played by Dreyfus is very much how I imagine You some of the time—beautiful, sad, wounded, tender, consoling, ultimately powerful. Mother may not be the right word at all—older lover whom one has known for a lifetime.

I shall be required to write another sonnet—God as older lover.

Are You really that way? Is Ms. Hepburn really a hint of what You're like? In one sense the answer to that is obvious. Everything good, true, and beautiful is a sacrament of You. But is she a special metaphor—the wise, beautiful, tender older woman? Is she a kind of pieta?

I rather think so. Obviously it is my religious sensibility, romantic as they come. But I hold with the insight that

235

You are a romantic which is why You made us a romantic. Therefore I can legitimately conclude that Audrey Hepburn as the fey, gentle, all-knowing romantic woman is an excellent metaphor for You.

At least in my life, which is what we are talking about, isn't it?

I'll treasure the image.

February 16

I READ the Psalms every day because priests have read them every day since almost the beginning. Yet I find myself wondering intermittently why I should read them. They are, with all respect, dreadfully dull—same old pity for self and railing against enemies and begging that You justify the psalmist's cause. Interesting examples of the religious imagination of the time perhaps, but how useful today when our images of You are, if not less anthropomorphic, at least more nuanced? Could we not put together a collection of Christian poems which would be more pertinent to our religious insights and needs today?

In a sense I envy the psalmist's simple vision of reality, one in which You punish the bad guys and reward the good guys and of course we are the good guys. For weal or woe I know that in this world virtue is not always rewarded and vice not always punished and that it is not legitimate to identify You with my cause, for to do so would be to succumb to the temptation to idolatry.

How much religious vigor seems to be lost in the change from his world view to mine. The fundamentalist always has more vigor and more self-confidence, even if he is an idolater.

One can always read the Psalms as deeper metaphors than the psalmists intended, translating their metaphors into ours, but that is a difficult work of piety and not, I think, the best way to go about praying.

Don't misunderstand me. I intend to go on praying the Psalms, but their inadequacy is another indicator of how much we need prayers that can speak out of our world view to You.

I guess we need religious geniuses in our day of the sort the psalmists were in their day and no one can mandate the appearance of genius.

February 19

IT'S snowing again, the fifth snowstorm this winter. Jack Shea is coming to visit after some lectures up in Phoenix. A house guest, even the least difficult of all the house guests in the world, when it's snowing in Arizona. And myself having gone to all the films in town!

The intent, my intent anyway, was to do responsible research and make it available in responsible fashion to a wide audience. That will not happen, not now at any rate. Maybe if we can scrape together the money for a later phase there'll be another chance.

Everything went wrong despite all the work. Why bother when there is always a good chance that it will all go wrong?

Even if we had been luckier was it worth all the effort, that's the big question just now. I've worked awfully hard throughout the years and to what purpose? If I had worked less hard and produced less and less controversial stuff I might have received more of a hearing for what I've done because I would not have stirred up so much envy.

As You can tell I'm in a glum mood. The snow dosen't help!

I'm frustrated and discouraged, not tired. And I feel somehow unclean because of all the junk that has come from the marriage study. If I had done less and avoided the public eye, I would not be tainted by this uncleanliness. If I had written a single scholarly book every five years it would be taken seriously, even by other priests.

Well, that's all foolish talk, because I didn't do it that way and couldn't and wouldn't even if I had a chance to do it again. It's useful to know that one's work is not all that important and that it matters a lot less than one thinks it does. But still one does what one can to the best of one's ability and that's that, regardless of what happens. We're put here by You for a time and we're expected to try hard. The twist is that we must try hard and yet maintain a certain distance from what we do. That's the challenge and one to which I have not responded all that well, though perhaps I'm improving—or just getting used to being battered and to failing. This failure on the marriage study is a good lesson. Success might have blinded me to how temporary are all things human.

Help me to work within the constraints of the dilemma—work hard and be detached (well, somewhat detached!) from the results.

February 20

SHEA and I saw the new *Henry V* last night. Very well done. It showed all the terrible ugliness of war. No, I take that back. Having read John Keegan's account of the Battle of Agincourt, I would say that the battle itself was much uglier. I have been reading Keegan's account of World War II, a book so horrific that You simply have to distance Yourself from the human suffering described in it to continue reading the book. I can remember most of the battles from the newspapers of those days. I was too young to think of the horror of all that death and maiming. If You suffer whenever one of us suffers, how much You must have suffered in all that gore. How much work You must have had to do to heal all the wounds to the human psyche. I do believe that not even a sparrow falls without Your concern, but, dear God, forty to fifty million deaths!

I guess I'm at the age in life where I believe in pacifism. I'm going to start writing columns against conscription because it is pretty clear that if the big powers don't have draft armies available to them, they're not able to fight wars.

Have mercy on those who die in combat, forgive them their sins, dry their tears, heal those who suffer the loss of loved ones and grant that the peace in Europe which seems to be coming about will mark the end of total wars of the sort which have blighted this century.

Andrew Greeley

February 21

I'VE finished reading the book on the war. It's an odd experience to recall an event which I witnessed as a kid and a teenager through the eyes of a half century of experience. Virtually no one younger than me in the world has a memory of the war as something that happened while they were alive—and of course my memory is newspaper, radio, and newsreel memory, not the more vivid memories of Europeans my age who lived through it.

I am astonished that so many people, especially Americans, have no sense of history about that event, no more recollection of it than they do of the Spanish Influenza. Only the most naive idiots can advocate the reunification of Germany, but in the absence of any historical sense most Americans are naive idiots.

Well, none of that seems especially pertinent for spiritual reflection. It's column material. However, there is surely reflection needed on the lesson that the human condition is tragic. Not only do we die, but we die ugly. Not only do we die, but most of our hopes and our expectations are susceptible to being blotted out by blind and unreasoning furies. Those of us who escape the furies are the fortunate ones indeed. That my life has not been troubled by the furies save those of envy is a blessing I do not deserve—but for which I assure You I am very grateful indeed. With images of the War in my head, I can't be nearly so concerned about the failure of the marriage study. Life is a precious gift, existing in a cosmic context that is mostly tragic and is certainly laden in the inevitability of death. I must value the gift itself and all its joys as the fragile graces they are.

Death of course is not the last word.

February 22

I'VE learned during the last two days that a couple to whom I was every close long ago have separated. That's the bad news. The good news is that they are both in individual therapy and also in joint therapy together. Please help them to make it. One of the mutual friends, himself a psychiatrist, said that he thinks they have a fifty/fifty chance. That's higher than I would put it, but they're going to need a lot of Your grace.

Please grant them the courage and the faith and the insight and the honesty they need. From my vantage point I have to say that I estimate their chances at a lot less than fifty/fifty. But then I would not have had much hope before now that they would come to this crisis point—and surely Your grace must have given them a good shove to come this far. Keep on shoving, I beg You.

You love them more than I ever did or ever could, so I guess my prayer to You about them this morning is merely to consign them to Your love.

February 23

MY LOVE,

I'm coming to the end of Matthew's Gospel. The Gospels are love stories with happy endings. What could be happier than a triumph of life over death, of love over hate? The good folks win and the bad folks lose, despite their schemes and machinations. If we abandon the search in the Gospels for proof-texts and moral obligations and read them as love stories they make a lot more sense— and we treat them and their authors with respect.

I confess I didn't get much out of Matthew this time around. I know the stories too well. I've read them too often. I'm too familiar with the exegetical analysis and not familiar enough with the literary analysis of the kind in which Shea is now engaged. Like the Psalms, it was written in and for a different era with different questions in mind and different concerns.

I suppose that the appropriate response to over familiarity with the Gospels is that the more one reads them the more one gets out of them. Maybe I'm jaded. Maybe I go too fast in my early morning spiritual reading. Or, more likely, I need a new approach. Maybe I need to concentrate more on them, though that doesn't seem to help. Anyway, as I begin Mark on Sunday I'll have to find some way to rejuvenate my gospel reading. Obviously I must try to integrate the gospel passage more closely into these reflections.

Today's passage is the answer in narrative to many of the concerns which have preoccupied me in the ten months I have been working on these reflections—the resurrection, the triumph of life over death, the down payment so to speak on the triumph of all of us over death. I believe in that triumph, though often I fear it is merely an intellectual conviction and not one which transforms my life.

My friend and colleague David Greenstone died the

other day, far too early in life. I will write his wife and mother-in-law this morning with my sympathy, a hard task because their religious tradition (rather at odds with the Talmud, I believe) does not accept life after death. I will hint at the possibility in my letters. I have an advantage in living (if not in writing to them) because I believe in survival. I can be confident that we will all be young again, we will all laugh again. But if such a conviction—and it is an authentic conviction, I don't doubt it for a moment—were to permeate and transform my life, there would be more joy and less weariness in it.

Help me to believe that death is really vanquished, that it has no more power over us. David and I will meet again.

February 24

Tor Books has agreed to publish the marriage report which means that with their advance I can go ahead with the second phase of the data collection. My worries about it were silly. I adjusted to the fact that they were silly and now the project is going ahead. No earthly project, no matter how important or how challenging, is worth more than a morning's worry at the most. I will survive nicely, as long as You give me time, regardless of what happens.

In any case, many thanks for the rebirth of this project. Help me to do a good job at it.

It's a beautiful Saturday morning here in Tucson, temperature heading towards 80, clear blue sky. In Chicago there's a forty mile-an-hour wind and temperature plunging towards zero. I'm glad I'm here. I'm sorry that the Tucson interlude is more than half over. Yet I'll be happy to return to Chicago.

I never said I was consistent, did I?

How have I used the Tucson time? I am certainly more relaxed and rested, though not as relaxed as I would have wished to be. I have however pretty much kept to my intention of not doing any serious work here. I am grateful for this interlude in my life. It's always a great blessing, one which I don't feel I deserve, though I will gladly take it.

Mark's Gospel begins this morning like the sound of a trumpet—an outline Gospel, a schema if one will, an announcement that the long expected Good News is not only at hand, but has actually happened and the human condition will never be the same. As pure prophecy that statement is certainly accurate. The coming of Jesus did indeed transform the human condition. The world has never been the same, although we have a long way to go before the vision of Jesus transforms the world the way it ought to.

It's a goal for which we should all labor—and here the reason for work which bothered me a couple of days ago returns. No one can expect to accomplish total transformation (that's 1960s perfectionism); but everyone must be able at the end of life to ask what s/he has done to make the world a better place—a question which takes into account the blessings and responsibilities that each of us has been given. I have been given a lot, I've done some things. Have I done enough, nearly enough?

The answer to that is easy: No.

Help me, please, to keep trying.

February 25

MARK, without much consideration of the preliminaries, plunges almost immediately into the public life of Jesus. It's hard, my Love, to recreate in one's mind the excitement which His preaching of the Good News must have stirred in those who heard it for the first time. There were of course other wandering preachers in that era, men with even wilder and more outrageous predictions. But there must have been something special about the preaching of Jesus or perhaps about the man who preached which attracted people and stirred up enthusiasm—confidence, goodness, intensity, charm, presence, some combination of all three?

Whatever it was, it must have been magical to have produced the results that followed. For us today, the good news so often seems old hat. We have heard it so often, read the Gospels so many times, pondered it and analyzed it so intensively that the freshness has worn off and the excitement long since slipped away.

We are not necessarily to be blamed for that. The process of what Max Weber called the routinization of the charisma is natural enough for us humans. The Church and often most of us are more concerned about our own ends, money, power, prestige, influence, than about the excitement of the gospel. The iron law of oligarchy as Michaels called it. We're all tired, as I am tired this cloudy Sunday morning in Tucson. It's hard to sustain enthusiasm when You're tired. Even revolutionaries have to sleep, they said in the sixties. Even enthusiasts get tired.

Andrew Greeley

What can I tell You.

As I read through Mark this winter-turning-into-spring, tired and growing old, battered and beaten and discouraged, help me to rediscover and recapture some of the enthusiasm of the old days.

February 26

I HAD an interesting experience yesterday. After supper with the Bishop and Tom and Leo, I went over to Our Mother of Sorrows to hear Leo give the first talk of his mission. He was, as I thought he would be, wonderful. As You well know he talked about You. He didn't go as far in his metaphors as I would but he was still very very impressive.

Tom's associate had found a book that I wrote eighteen years ago in a stack of old books someone had left at the rectory: *A Touch of the Spirit,* remember that? I picked it up and began to read it. It was an uncanny experience. Somehow it brought back that whole era of my life. Moreover the words I had written were both mine and a stranger's. The thoughts were mine, and in some respects they haven't changed much since then. But the style was different than anything I could write today—simpler, more confident, perhaps more direct and powerful. It was based on a series of columns on spirituality I had done for the *National Catholic Reporter.* Maybe that was why the style was different from my *Mail Box Parish* letter, which oddly dealt with some of the same things as in this issue. Or, more likely, I have changed since then. I realize the world is more complicated than it seemed when I was in my middle forties and I have less confidence in myself. Also it was written before I began to do fiction which has had a profound effect I think on my nonfiction.

And of course the spiritual ideas in the book have now become embodied in my fiction. As I remember, almost no one bought the book. Yet the ideas seemed fresh and alive. I guess even by then the relevant audience had turned me off because I wrote too much. So it wasn't the fiction which did it, though it certainly offended them even more. It's a book which ought to be reissued, like *Complaints Against God.*

Anyway, in Mark this morning Jesus has begun to work signs of the presence of God in the world. That's what a priest should be doing. That's what Leo was doing last night. That's what I've tried to do all my life, sometimes with more success than other times. Help me to continue to do it to the best of my ability and not be distracted by the foolish fights in which I become involved.

I guess this is a prayer for a little more personal peace than I've ever had, especially since I've started to write and people, especially priests and clerical culture laity, started to assault me for what I had written and even more for the fact that I have written.

Grant me more peace and with the peace more power in preaching You.

February 27

THE stories in Mark continue to be about healing, a sign of God's presence in the world as revealed in the works of Jesus. I reflect again on my own role as a healer. I know I have healed many people through my stories, more indeed than everything else I did in the priesthood put together. Odd, isn't it, that my most healing work should also cause the most conflict and pain for me and the most animosity for the critics. Healing and fury created by the same work.

Help me because I need healing. Otherwise I will become not only old, which is all right because it is part of the wisdom You plan for all of us, but cynical which is not all right at all.

February 28

ASH WEDNESDAY

As if You knew that I needed reassurance yesterday, You inundate me with it—a positive, very positive reaction to my talk at Our Mother of Sorrow about Catholic schools, the book of letters about my novels that June sent me and a good review of my religious change book in the *American Journal of Sociology*. These reactions should convince me that there are other responses to my work out there in the world. Or to talk in terms of Mark my efforts at revealing Your healing love have not been totally unsuccessful.

Of course I know that. The events of yesterday merely served to confirm what I ought never to have forgotten. People do listen and do agree. I can't expect unanimous acclamation.

The problem is that I don't value enough the positive

feedback and permit the negative feedback to get to me. In principle that's not so bad either because there is little danger that the positive feedback will give me a big head. But I should at least take it as evidence that the envious critics are wrong and systematically so.

As I try to consider this serious problem in my life, it dawns on me that when the negative stuff piles up, I'm inclined to think that maybe they're right. I wonder if I have enough confidence in my novels against the carping voices. Only when I read a favorable review or a positive essay from one of the scholars who is specializing in my work do I begin again to treat my stories with the respect to which they are entitled from their creator before anyone else.

I know that my sociology is skillful and that there is no one in sociology of religion who can do what I do routinely. Yet in the face of the nasty critics I guess I forget that—until I read something like the review in the *American Journal of Sociology* yesterday, for which I am very grateful to You, as well as to the reviewer, by the way.

I guess this is the special temptation to discouragement of the writer and the scholar. I may lack the arrogance to believe strongly that my work is good no matter what anyone says. Again I suspect that such a lack is probably a good thing. But somehow I should be able to occupy a middle ground where I value my work but am open to learning about how to improve it. Finding that middle ground has been no easy task.

I'll keep trying, which is all that You expect.

Why don't I value my work enough? That's a question to return to tomorrow when I am less tired than I am on this Ash Wednesday. It's an important question which I have never asked myself—yet another sign that I don't really respect my own work adequately.

March 1

WHERE did February go so quickly?

Anyway, to the subject I promised to reflect on today— why I don't value my own work enough. I have always said to young people that the secret of writing was to distance Your selfhood from the work, so that the work did not have to be perfect and the worth of the self was not equated with the outcome of the work. That is surely true. If my personhood was identified with my writing in my own mind I would have stopped writing long ago. Not only me, I might add, but every writer whose productivity and/or success stirs up the envious. Only the distance between who I am and what I write enables me (or any writer) to go on.

Now it seems as I reflect on this subject that there is a downside to this distancing: a book or an article becomes unimportant if there is too much of a distance between self and product. I maintain a great distance between me and my work. When something is done it is done. I rarely read a novel or a non-fiction book or even an article after it's published. I certainly don't exult in the act of holding a published copy in my hands. Thus when a critic says that something its worthless or worse than worthless, one part of me thinks that probably there is an element of truth in what the critic says. If I have done something quickly and know that it is imperfect (like every human effort) and have maintained a great distance between it and myself, I am not likely to have such a high opinion of it. I am almost surprised when a critic gives a generous review as the man did in the *American Journal of Sociology* article yesterday or as some of the academic critics do when they write about my novels. Maybe, I tell myself, the work is worth more than I thought it was.

I wonder if I have a high opinion of anything I have ever done. That it is really important, really something to be proud of—these are emotions I don't feel and I've never felt and perhaps I never will feel.

This puzzles me a lot.

March 2

YESTERDAY was a terrible day. Come to think of it, this week has been a terrible week. I've had migrane headaches twice—and often I don't have them in the course of a whole year. Three manuscripts showed up the same day with copy editing. And all week, especially yesterday, the phone rang from seven-thirty till I left for supper and a concert. I was a basket case. The phone calls were especially bad, people keeping me on the phone for forty-five minutes and others just refusing to let me go. I suppose, as I reflect on it now, the combination of the minute details required for copy editing and the constant interruption of attention to those details by the clanging phone were the causes of my tension which I fear ruined lunch, supper, and the concert for me and probably was not unnoticed by my hosts.

Andrew Greeley

I was terrible, I must admit, just terrible.

I don't know how to handle such days. Obviously there is not a conspiracy for everyone to call me. Obviously there is not a conspiracy to send three copy-edited texts to me at the same time. Yet on days like yesterday, indeed on weeks like this, the notion that I am in Tucson for rest and relaxation seems so absurd.

I guess it might be said that I have too many irons in the fire and therefore it is certain that some days will be as bad as yesterday, some weeks as bad as this week and the trick is to roll with the punch. I admit the truth of this observation, but yesterday the harassment was so unceasing that it almost seemed demonic.

What offends me in particular is that each caller seems to feel that s/he has an unlimited right to my time. Even when one asks me if I'm busy the only tolerated answer is "no." I suppose I could have turned the fax and the phone off, but there were some important calls I was expecting in the midst of all the foolishness.

I don't think I've been under so much pressure all winter long. Internally produced pressure? I guess so. I don't have to react so fiercely to phone calls. Yet I could not even get the packages out of the car when I came home from the store yesterday before I had two phone calls, one of them long. Both of them frivolous and foolish.

I had to cut my swimming time short because of all the phone calls. That sounds selfish but You know how much I need to swim if I am not to become tense.

Well, I failed—as I don't have to tell You. And this morning I'm still a wreck, exhausted, tense, angry, tense for the calls to begin again.

I can't cope with any of this just now. My anger is irrational but I still feel it. Small wonder I have to get up at 5:00 to write. The phone callers (and the fax senders) are consuming my life.

If I can climb down off this high of tension and anger —or better when I climb down—I'll have to try to devise a rational response. I'm sorry for dumping this all on You, but what are lovers for if not to listen to cries of pain and frustration?

The phone just rang, beginning today's harassment. Another invitation for dinner.

Won't it ever stop.

Help me to relax.

March 4

IT continues to be a bad week. Even on Friday and Saturday, the phone rings when I'm getting out of the car to come into the house or when I sit down to read the *New York Times*. This was supposed to be a week for rest and relaxation and it has been hellish, in part because of the three manuscripts which arrived for revision on Wednesday, but also because of the endless ringing of the phone. I'm at a loss as to how to respond to it. The revisions will be done before today is over, but will next week be as bad? I fervently hope not, but, given the number of my involvements, I really can't control that.

I thought I'd be free from dinners this coming week. Now I'm stuck with three invitations and two for lunch —none of which I instigated and none of which I want.

I really don't know what to do, I really don't.

The result of all of this is that I don't have any peace

or any time to admire the beauty of the desert. I might just as well be in Chicago in the clouds and cold. Today will be another bad day I fear, time slipping away with obligations that I'd rather not have.

I could also cut out some of my projects or diminish them in the weeks and months to come. I could conclude that after the present sociology is finished there will be no more sociology. I'll just write stories which would be more fun. But I like the sociology and would not want to have to give it up. Besides even if I quit sociology, the phone wouldn't stop ringing.

I don't know what the answer is. I do know that I can't keep up the way this last week has been—a week be it noted which, when it started, looked free of harassments and turned into one of the worst of my life.

Who needs a week in Arizona when my head throbs at the end of every day?

Well one practical conclusion. I will not answer the phone when I'm trying to work on something or revise something. Let it ring, regardless.

Help me, please. Or to be respectful and accurate, help me to help myself.

March 5

THE beginning of a new week. I'm still worn out from last week but beginning to feel better. Last night coming home from seeing *Glory* and obsessed with carnage and death I began to wonder whether I was going to die. I don't mean eventually, but soon. I was so tired and so depressed and so discouraged. A good night's sleep made me feel better. A day or two of relative inaction and another couple of good nights of sleep should help. I can't figure out yet what happened—other than the three manuscripts coming the same day last week, which would have been enough to disturb anyone.

I take it all as a warning, however, that I ought to be wary of these situations when the world seems to close in. When they happen I should take charge immediately, and maybe do some self-hypnotism to slow down. I thought of that this time, but was too busy to even try the self-hypnotism!

Dumb!

Anyway, this week looks less hectic. I must not let it get hectic! Please Help me! You did not mean for me to live the way I lived last week. Life was not designed for that kind of frustration.

If I am to be a healer in imitation of Your son about whose gentle healing I am reading in Mark's Gospel, I have to be healed somewhat myself. I can't live and act the way I did last week.

I hope that today and the rest of this week give me a chance to reorient myself in that direction.

Again I ask, please help me.

March 6

THIS should be a pretty good day, no lunch or supper. We'll see tomorrow whether I'll be able to use it to catch up.

The poem I managed to read this morning while the phone was ringing offered some beautiful images about the wonders of the time between sleeping and waking, the time when we're all poets. Since I'm a poet and a storyteller (of a sort anyway) this time of imagery and indeed all times of imagery should be important. But perhaps that is not strong enough. Simply as a human being, imagery times are important to a fully human life— otherwise You wouldn't have made us image-creating beings (another call, the ninth so far). Which is to say the evolutionary process would not have selected for our image-generating capabilities.

I was rereading some of Chesterton's stories yesterday and was impressed again by his remarkable metaphoric abilities. I am not GKC and my metaphors need not be like his. But I can create my own metaphors when I have the time and the freedom. I don't permit myself enough of either. I don't grant myself the opportunity to wallow, as it were, in the delightfully warm and richly scented swamp where the preconscious temporarily connects the flows of the conscious and the unconscious, where it's high water for the the latter and low water for the former so that the unconscious flows through the swamp of the preconscious into the conscious.

I know from experience how soothing that experience is, how much peace and insight come from it. It's the answer to fighting off the phones and the harassments. I must try to do it sometime today and every day if I can.

These reflections, as important to me as they have become, are mostly cognitive and propositional. That's good, but that's not enough. Time in the swamp is necessary to slow down the pace of life and to establish deeper and more regular contact with my other self, the poet who rushes into action when given half a chance to do do so.

Help me and protect me this day. Let me understand as in the wonderful story of the sower in Mark's Gospel which I read this morning that the fearsome and benign energy which You have set free in the world (and which Jesus calls Your kingdom) is sweeping all before it and that my own work is important to the success of that energy, but never so important that I must work myself into a frazzle because of my contribution. Help me, in other words, to rely comfortably and confidently on that energy.

March 7

LADY WISDOM

(Based on Audrey Hepburn as God in the film *Always*)

When you wake up from surgery, a skillful nurse—
Compassionate, sensitive—a distant light,
A promise of peace and reassurance,
A loving mother to tuck you in at night.
No longer is there any need to hide,
All is seen and long ago remitted
A sympathetic judge, a case already tried
And a verdict given—"you're acquitted!"
She's not a great accountant in the sky
Nor an old monsignor with a walking cane

Andrew Greeley

Who waits to chase us quickly off to hell,
But a long-loved spouse who wipes away our pain
And draws us to her breasts that we may cry—
In her embrace things always turn out well.

This "God Sonnet" was one of the easiest to write, perhaps because it had been lurking in my preconscious for
a long time, perhaps because of the power of the image
in Always and perhaps because I have been fascinated
lately by the power of the attraction between older people
who are very much in love with one another and deeply
attracted to one another sexually. It occurred to me that
the experienced and familiar and delightful spouse might
be another image of You—even for someone who never
had a spouse but was capable of imagining such a person.

My images of You seem always to be passionate and
affective and intimate. Each time I write one of these
poems I tell myself that I ought to try one in which You
are less, how shall I say, reassuring, more fearsome, more
a judge, more a God of the parables of urgency instead
of the God of the parables of reassurance. Somehow my
imagination can't work on that, though the next one will
be on Your kingdom which I will see as an enormous
energy of love, as Your son Jesus saw it—or at least as
I see him seeing it!

If the fear of You is the beginning of wisdom, I must
say there is not much fear in my Lady Wisdom poem.
Perhaps my unease is in part the result of the imagery
of my grammar school days which thinks these later images are not respectful enough, perhaps a little blasphemous.

The poems are all metaphors of course and as such

incomplete as well as inadequate. They are the images which serve me best now and lurk most powerfully in my imagination, which is all that matters. I'll do a few more and then consider publishing them somewhere as a kind of theological statement.

Yesterday morning was at least as bad as anything before. It was towards the end of the day that I was able to get control of my life and work on the poem which was a tremendously reassuring experience. I simply have to do it more.

Also I have to swim in the morning because that too calms me down and protects me from the phone which can't get at me in the pool.

March 8

IT'S noontime on a relatively quiet day. I was distracted early in the morning by a few calls and then decided I would swim. The best strategy for me to cope, however, is to write these reflections and swim before the phone starts ringing. That would mean I should get up earlier, which I am loathe to do here in Tucson.

Since my last reflection, I've had to once again go through my book with the rabbi. The materials there on the scripture are very good indeed. The same with the book on the Spirit which started this series of reflections in the first place.

I was astonished at how good both works are. Is that not odd? Someone who doesn't value his own work highly enough until he is forced for one reason or another to read it again?

Andrew Greeley

I suppose that because so much of my work is done on the run and for specific purposes and goals and because it flows so easily I do not put enough value on it—or in the talent with which You have blessed me.

That's pretty stupid, isn't it?

What comes out of this, other than a little more self-understanding—is a sense of gratitude and responsibility to You?

I suppose the most important conclusion is that I should value and respect that which You have given me far more than I do and not let myself be disturbed by those who must distort so that they can hate. I must also find comfort and reassurance in the knowledge that I am doing something that is good and important, no matter what others say.

I should have made that explicit in my head long ago. There is enough evidence of it in the favorable reaction (especially in the letters about the novels) to which I pay so little attention.

March 9

The Kingdom of God
(FOR LEO MAHON)

"The Kingdom of God is at hand!"
Not heaven's city of God, ivory and gold,
Nor a spired Byzantium here on earth,
A theocracy biblical and old,
Benignly ruled by goodly king and pious pope.
But a raging torrent, smashing through the ice

YEAR OF GRACE

To rush in lethal flood madly towards the sea,
A firestorm that consumes and devastates,
A blood red furnace spilling molten steel.

A dangerous demanding dynamism,
Yet somehow winsome—the famished divine
Desire unleashed, that is the kingdom of God!
The Creator's lustful fervor arisen,
A tumultuous, delicate hurricane—
The rapacious love of God falls upon the world!

I don't know whether You will like it or not. No, I take that back. You will like it. What I really mean is that I think many Catholics would find it almost blasphemous. Yet it certainly fits the data from the Bible and from the tradition and from the parables of Jesus (as I will try to work out in my next sonnet). The kingdom of God is an awesome energy of Your power (which is to say Your love) set loose in the world, probably from the instant of creation and accelerating through the billions of years until it reached fever pitch in the present.

Again I speak of You in metaphors, even in the last sentence. But how else to speak of You? The poem is based on Leo's talk about the "kingdom" and Shea's imagery of the kingdom as an energy sweeping the world. You as a rapist? Well, You know what I mean—a frantic lover, but also as I say winsome and delicate. As I have often said the image of the lover so sexually aroused as to be almost out of control fails when applied to You by defect: it is not strong enough in its depiction of Your passion.

It was time for me to write about Your power and

energy. The other sonnets in the cycle miss that dimension of You. One can't say everything at the same time, indeed one can't say everything about You in all times. But I am also aware in my imagination of Your strength —creation is not just a teenage dance.

I don't doubt these images. I certainly don't deny them. Yet they are not my favorites, as You well know. The ones I like the best are the images of You as a vulnerable lover.

How reconcile those with the images in today's sonnet?

I don't have to reconcile them because You're God and all metaphors apply to the infinite without being contradictions.

March 10

WHAT am I to make of the story in Mark this morning of the Geresene Demoniac? I have told congregations that I don't know what to make of it, which seems to relieve them because it seems to baffle them too.

Mark has taken a folktale about Jesus which must have floated around in the tradition and included it in the gospel as a sign of Jesus' cures and healing—which we now know were not so much intended to be a proof as a sign of the triumph of good over evil, of healing over punishment. At that level, fair enough, I guess. My problem in reading it is the "proof text" approach which demanded, even in the time of the patristic commentaries, that some deeper meaning be found in the story— and of course to argue that it is an event which actually happened the way it is narrated. Perhaps there is a germ of a historical incident in the tale, the cure of a psychotic which happened at the same time a bunch of pigs went mad.

I suppose that when we worry about what the story really means we miss the obvious meaning—the kingdom of God, that loving fury I tried to describe in metaphor with my last poem, is sweeping through the world with ever greater intensenity, healing the sick and the troubled.

Surely the ability of medicine to cure and to prolong life has grown enormously since the time of Jesus. Is that improvement part of the kingdom of God? Don't we have to say that it is? That it all fits into the goals of the irresistible energy which is bent on continuing the work of transformation begun in the act of creation?

This view of the coming of the kingdom sanctifies all human effort to make the world a better place and to improve the lot of humans—even when the work itself seems small and insignificant it is part of the coming of the kingdom.

So on this Saturday morning, tired, but not as tired as I was at the end of last week, I can see the work ahead of me in my remaining two weeks in Tucson as part of the coming of the kingdom.

Only two weeks left and they're going to be crowded. My intent to rest and relax has been only partially successful. I suppose that is part of the destiny of my life. At least I had some rest. I don't like the picture of April and May which lies ahead, of lots of work, lots of traveling, lots of harassment.

So help me to squeeze as much relaxation as possible into the next two weeks, especially this weekend.

Andrew Greeley

March 11

The God of the Parables

An indulgence no parent could defend—
Warm welcome to a fawning, worthless son;
A day's pay for those mumbling at the end
From a silly farmer when day's work is done;
A woman whose sins all right minds offend,
Her forgiveness from the judge quickly won;
A man whom no one will befriend
Finds himself redeemed by a Samaritan.

O God of Jesus, you're quite round the bend,
By human folly not to be outdone.
What sort of crazy message do You intend?
By what madness do You propose to stun?
"The big surprise you cannot comprehend?
The triumph of My love has just begun!"

I hope You like this, the eighth of my "God Sonnets."
That's the last of them for a while. Poems, as You know,
can be mass-produced. In this one I accomplished what
I set out to do, namely jam together the images of the
four parables to increase the force of the contrast between the one surprised and the nature of the surprise.
It's hard after listening for much of one's life to moralistic
or allegorical interpreations of the parables to return to
their original parabolic, that is surprise, meanings. The
task is not made any easier by some (not all) of the serious
scholars of the parables who must play their own little

deconstructionist or quasi-deconstructionist games with them. That they are designed to surprise and disconcert ought to be clear from the very beginning.

But I don't live or act like a surprised person, like one whose surprise is so overwhelming that it contages from him to others. I try, which may be more most priests of my age and my generation do, but I have yet a long way to go, especially when I am hassled and harassed, as I expect to be all next week.

March 12

THE gospel passage this morning (and I've already done my swim according to my promise) is the charming story of the daughter of Jairus. I remember the arguments we used in the seminary to prove that the little girl was in fact dead and not just asleep as Jesus said she was. The arguments, like most such, were irrelevant. Dead or asleep she was about to be buried, so Jesus saved her life, one way or another; and that's what counts, not whether he worked a special kind of miracle.

More appealing—and almost certainly part of the original tradition because the Evangelists were not given to noting such details—was Your son's admonition that they had better give her something to eat because she was hungry. (Incidentally, since the metabolistic processes stop in a corpse, this comment alone shows that Jesus didn't think she was really dead.) I strongly suspect that Jesus was a kid freak just the way I am. Good for both of us, says I.

Mark in this whole section of the gospel is driving

home with great vigor the message that Jesus came to heal, while at the same time displaying great care so that Jesus doesn't work vast numbers of miracles as the other wonder workers of the era were alleged to do. The miracles were the signs of God's healing love unleashed in the ever growing kingdom of heaven, described in my sonnet of a couple of days ago. They are a challenge to me as a priest responsible in a special way for proclaiming the message of the kingdom to also be a healer. I've been through the reasons why sometimes I do not heal all that well and there's no need to repeat them today. I must strive nonetheless to be a healer even when I am angry and find myself under assault of the envious and the haters. I have struck back in anger too many times.

I note that in the new awareness of envy (articles in the *NYT* for example) that they almost never provide advice to those envied on how they should respond. Even now the envious are the concern of the scholars. Those who are assaulted received no sympathy—almost as if they deserved to be attacked.

March 13

MY LOVE,

Just when I wonder why I am reading that book of best American poems of 1988 I come across one that makes the whole book worthwhile—a poem by Theialis Moss about You. It's wonderful, so much better than my poor efforts. She belongs in the collection and, alas, I never will.

YEAR OF GRACE

She says in the comments in the back of the book that it is the final step in her reconciliation with You, whom she no longer sees as the Baptist God of her childhood. The image is the same as that of Rabbi Heschel (though she probably does not know the Rabbi's work), the pathos of God. She pictures You as worn out by the efforts of Your love and consoled in Your weariness by an angel who is the narrator of the poem. The angel is kind of a spouse who feels sorry for You and loves You as a good friend.

Now, obviously neither she nor I really think intellectually that You are worn out. But the only way we can imagine Your enormous work and enormous love is to see it as wearisome. A mother is wearied by one child, worn by two and exhausted by three. How many billions do You have in this planet alone? And in the whole cosmos? And in all the other cosmoi? And what about the birds who flit around the pool when I do my early morning swim? Does not Your Son say that You care for each one of them?

Who wouldn't be weary and discouraged?

You wouldn't in one sense, but in another sense I return to the truth that You cry when the little baby weeps and the image of the angel who is Your friend consoling You at the end of a frustrating day makes a lot of sense.

I'm that angel, or should be. You need my support and consolation. You need my arms around You to sustain You in Your work. That metaphor goes beyond anything Ms. Moss dares, but it is a valid and very Catholic metaphor. Would that I did more than just accept it.

Would that it permeated my life. At a minimum any time I read of human suffering, I can feel sorry not only for the humans but for You who suffer with them.

This is deep stuff and theologically difficult, I suppose, but it is scripturally valid and metaphorically accurate. Help me, my worn and weary Love, to absorb the image into my life and thus to transform it.

March 14

A LOT about angels these last couple of days. Last night I watched the film *Wings of Desire* about a couple of angels who were weary of spending eternity going around doing good for people, a theme not unlike that in the poem on which I reflected yesterday. Unlike my Gabriella, however, they weren't very energetic or resourceful angels. One of them decides to become human (at the invitation of Peter Falk-Columbo, who apparently had been one of them) and the color of the film changes from black and white to glorious color—the human world being a world of color unlike the angel world which is dull black and white.

So the final theme is different from that of the Moss poem and of course literally it is one I cannot accept. For any angel worth the name—and to be worth the name they must be something like my Gabriella—the world will be even more colorful than it is for us humans. However the point of the story, and it was often a weird, abstract German story (set in Berlin) is that to be human is to be glorious. Humans live in a world of color and taste and feel and smell and touch and human love. They drink coffee and eat sandwiches and embrace little kids and kiss one another in love. Angels, the protagonist says at the end of the film, cannot know the love between man and woman.

Well, they know a love that is better in my theory of angels, which I think is the traditional one in this respect. Moreover, Gabriella says that there is sexual differentiation in angels, too, so they know sexual love—God (You) forbid that I would disagree with Gabriella, especially since as You well know she is a sacrament of You.

However, humans do know the love between man and woman and whether it's worse or better than the love between and among angels is irrelevant, even, I think, to the filmmaker who wanted to celebrate the marvels of the human condition and to reawaken the viewers to those marvels. Angels are a plot device, as I think they are in Moss's poems.

My angels, if You pardon me for mentioning them again, are not plot devices, they are sacraments.

Anyway, it's a clear day here as spring struggles to return and the desert and the mountains and the trees and the cacti are filled with Your grace and charm and beauty. Unlike the protagonist in the film I don't emerge from black and white to full color. I live in full color all the time and hardly notice it. I barely listen to the birds or relish the taste of Earl Grey tea or melons or savor the smell of creosote after a storm or revel in the calm night air here after dinner. I am so busy with my own efforts that I do not take time to enjoy Your efforts.

So my next sonnet will be about God the artist, the underappreciated artist. In the meantime, help me to be more aware of and more grateful for Your wondrous world.

March 15

THE last couple of days have been quiet, not many calls, no lunch or dinner obligations, a time for reading and watching films and doing what I came here to do—rest and relax. It takes only a couple of days like that for me to feel refreshed again. Moreover my resolution to swim and do these reflections (and my spiritual reading the night before) has worked pretty well. I have been faithful to my commitment not to answer the phone if it rings before nine o'clock (and the first one in the last few days is ringing right now: let it ring, says I). There's nothing I can do about the fax which started buzzing at 6:45 and already has three messages. I won't respond to them till after nine either.

One of the reasons that this is hard is that I've spent much of my life believing that a priest ought to be accessible whenever the phone rings. That denies the priest all privacy. In any case, I am not a parish priest waiting for sick calls and I need not be accessible all the time.

You understand what I mean when I say that this is a difficult change to make and, like I say however silly it may be, important for my life. It took me a long time to keep the phone away from the pool. Now I must resolve not to answer it when I'm engaged in something that it will interrupt.

If it's important, they'll call back. If it's not, look at the time and the money I've saved both of us!

The story in Mark is the tale of the death of John the Baptist, which will forever be associated in my mind with the Richard Strauss opera that the Lyric did last year. John, it often is said, died because he was a religious fanatic. Surely he was more vigorous in his denunciations than Jesus was—though in the long run Jesus' moderation did not make any difference. But the envy of the priests and the leader was at least as important in bringing about John's death as was Herod's idiot pride and Herodias's revenge.

I conclude that it's a dangerous world for those who speak the truth—even in and about the Church. How could I have ever thought otherwise?

So, without being as bloody-minded as David is in the Psalms, I nonetheless beg You to protect me from my enemies and, even more, from false friends.

March 16, St. Paddy's Eve

MY LOVE,

To celebrate the day I went off last night to see the film *My Left Foot* about Christy Brown, the Irish writer who was born with cerebral palsy and learned to paint and write with the toes of his left foot.

The story is well known, almost a cliche about the human spirit. Yet, particularly with Daniel Day Lewis as Christy, it is a deeply moving and impressive story. One could draw many conclusions from it, particularly the importance of the Irish Catholic faith of Christy's family.

However, I want to reflect on Your strange ways of

manifesting Your power and love. Christy is obviously
a lesson to all of us, especially in my case of someone
who finds it difficult to write with the phone ringing all
the time. How much more difficult if I had only my left
foot with which to write. Would I have the courage of
a Christy Brown? Probably not. Or probably. How can
I tell? As my mother used to say God shapes the back
to fit the burden. Only a lot of backs don't seem adequate
to the burden placed on them.

Christy is a genius who was imprisoned temporarily
in a twisted body. How many other people (apparently)
have only twisted bodies. How many kids like Tommy
Brennan were not healed by family love, not because of
the lack of love but because their problems were so much
worse even than Christy's.

I don't know why some humans have to struggle harder
than others. I don't know why some lives seem destroyed
even before they are born. I don't know why some writers
are blessed, as I seem to be, with an almost fatal facil-
ity, physical and mental. I do know that You love all of
us and that the courage of Christy Brown reveals Your
presence in the world. I guess I have to say, in line with
my reflections earlier in this journal, that You don't want
anyone to have cerebral palsy and that You suffer with
all those who suffer with broken bodies or minds and
that You rejoice with all those who triumph over
handicaps.

And I guess I must add that You are disappointed in
those of us who have few handicaps and still complain.
I admire Christy Brown and his family, I am grateful for
their example. I am grateful that I have been protected
from such obstacles. I'm sorry I've ever complained

about the obstacles I encounter. I will continue to struggle against my own obstacles as best I can without complaint.

I do reserve the right to talk to You about them, but without complaint. If ever again I sound like I'm complaining, consider the complaint inoperative.

Thank You for the film. Tomorrow I turn to the miracle of the loaves and fishes.

March 17, St. Patrick's Day

MY article in the *National Catholic Reporter* on the Eucharist as story appeared yesterday with the reference to *Babette's Feast* as a eucharistic story. It will be interesting to see the reaction because I said that the Eucharist as story must, like all stories, be entertaining. That will be too much for the puritan liturgists.

It was a nice coincidence with my Saint Patrick's party last night which was a great event.

The point towards which I am struggling on the morning after is that there was a lot of food left over, as there always is when Carlotta caters a Mexican-Irish meal for me. On the one hand, with memories of the Irish famines in my head and the presence of near famines in the newspaper headlines the waste of food seems terrible. On the other, in the parable of the loaves which I read yesterday, there was a lot of food left over. Eucharist means an abundance of food it would seem. *Babette's Feast* would seem to the Marxist-oriented liturgical ideologues a horrendous waste. So it would have seemed to the hungry Irish during the famine.

Andrew Greeley

I finessed the issue last night by sending the food back with Carlotta who would find someone who needed it. But that doesn't solve the problem does it?

People do not go hungry in the world because we Americans eat well, despite some of the liberation theology types. They go hungry because of bad market systems. Our parents did not tell us the truth when they tried to motivate us to eat our suppers lest we be responsible for the starving children in (fill in whatever the name was in a given time, China in my time, Ethiopia today). In fact, the two were and are unrelated phenomena. We ought not to waste food because it is a gift and gifts should not be wasted.

Moreover one needs more than enough food for a good party and the party last night, as I said and as You know, was a wonderful party. Doug McAdam insisted that I tell stories which I did for a half hour and with considerable success—even Jim Coleman's eyes were as wide as a little kid's. The mix of food and stories and stories by a priest at that, made it a eucharistic way of celebrating St. Paddy's day. For which much thanks to You because parties don't always work out that way.

And thanks, too, that the Irish are no longer starving and that they have at last found comfortable lives in many parts of the world and even in Ireland itself. Help them in the old country break out of the cycle of depression in which they're caught so that their young people do not have to migrate and thank You that my ancestors did migrate. While I am also grateful to be Irish (a terrible thing to be until You consider the alternative) I am even more grateful to be Irish American.

I'm also grateful that, despite the negative stereotypes,

the Irish are still on the side of the oppressed, as I tried to prove in my letter to the *Times Book Review* last week. May we always be there.

Finally, protect us all this day when far too much of the drink is taken, for which also forgive us. And protect us through the year too. And grant that the Irish will somehow always remain Irish. It would not be the world it is if they should try to give up on what they are.

March 18

WHY were you afraid, Jesus demands of the apostles as he walks on the water. The answer, not to put too fine an edge on it, was that they were afraid of death. So are we. So am I. So is everyone.

You must understand that it is inevitable that we be afraid of death. As the only creature (of which we are aware) that knows it must die, we are doomed to fear death all the time—from the first moment we learn about it as little children until the last breath we take. To pretend that we are not afraid of death is to engage in deception—of ourselves or others or both.

All our other fears are rooted in this fear of death, as are many of our other vices. Envy, lust, greed, for example, each in its own way, is a flight from death. Existentially, fear of death is Original Sin, the desire of a contingent creature to be absolute, of a mortal creature to be immortal.

The poignancy, the glory, the tragedy, even the comedy of the human condition are based on our fear of dying.

Andrew Greeley

So Your son could hardly have expected the apostles not to be frightened in the lake storm. His gentle rebuke meant that they ought to have had more confidence in him. Would the One who multiplied the loaves and fishes permitted them to die eternally?

On a more general level, would You, who created us out of passionate love, permit us to perish?

This can easily be dismissed as wish-fullfillment, can it not? Because we don't want to die we create for ourselves the image of a God who loves us so much that She won't let us die.

Except the fact that we wish it were true does not make it false. The question remains open. Moreover, how explain the fact of our existence if creative love is removed from the picture. I don't mean here the strict philosophical argument; I mean rather the sign of grace we find in our own existence.

Anyway, I am a bundle of fears like all humans are. Generally they don't stop me from doing what needs to be done, but they do blight my life to some considerable extent. When I permit that to happen, I am forgetting about Your love.

I don't want to die. I'll never be ready to die. Well, maybe I will if my last agony is prolonged enough. But I accept death as part of the deal and believe that Your love is as strong as death, even stronger. Strengthen my faith in Your love.

March 19

I'VE already begun packing to go home on Friday. Tomorrow is the last day of winter. How the time has slipped away. I have been thinking that I don't really know how much difference this winter interlude in Tucson had made in my life during the last eleven years. I came here because I was tired of being an academic entrepreneur and because it was a good department whose invitation would cancel out the Chicago rejection and because there were parishes here where I could say Mass. I didn't pay much attention either way to the weather. Now the first three reasons are invalid but I still come because of friends and because I like to teach. Again the weather doesn't make that much difference in my conscious plans. But I suspect that the mild winter (though Chicago was mild this winter and the weather here has been none too good) is important both for my life and health.

Your crooked lines at work once again!

As always, I am sorry to leave. To leave what? The friends especially, the warmth and the casualness of the place. But I know that as soon as I am back home in Chicago I'll be delighted. Chicago is after all the place where I belong, isn't it?

Yet, as I made clear when I wrote my memoir, Tucson has been and still is a healing experience in my life. Thank You for the healing which continues even to the present. Despite some bad times this year, and especially that one bad week, this year has been a healing experience too.

Time slips away as it always does in human life. I'm grateful for the time You have given me and I'll do my best to honor and love You in the time that remains.

March 20

THE first day of spring and election day in Chicago. My temptation to turn the means into ends is to make my writing, fiction and non-fiction alike, into an end in itself, to become so involved in what I write and so concerned about the reaction to it that I forget that I write as a priest and with priestly goals. My stories are stories of You, my sociology is a study of religion for the purposes of the Catholic community (even though the official leadership of the community disdains my work), my presence in the sociological and journalist community is a priestly presence, representing if not the official church at least the organized Catholic community. I have, to put the best possible face on my failures, not always lived up to those goals.

The work itself usually measures in pretty well. Surely my stories are parables of Your Love. My work as a sociologist is what it ought to be. My journalistic commentary is almost always from a specific, if not explicit, priestly viewpoint.

It's my own attitudes and values, my loss of sight of the goals, my focus on the immediate problems, my failure to be a priestly presence, my concern for the details of publication and promotion.

Help me.

I'll be back tomorrow with more reflections on this subject. Right now I'm on overload which I ought not to be on the first day of spring with the temperature going towards 90.

March 21

SPRING came into Tucson yesterday with 92-degree heat. As You know from my past, the lengthening of the days after Christmas is a major event for me and the turn to spring an even more important event. I understand that it is nothing more than the result of the earth's orbit and the peculiar tilt it has on its axis—strictly small-time stuff to the physicists and astronomers. In the world of great cosmic mysteries it faded from importance long ago. All the poetry and the music and the romance results from a very minor phenomenon of orbital mechanics.

Yet I wonder if when You decided that there would be an evolutionary process on this tiny planet which would lead to rational life, You also decided that there would be a tilt to the axis of the planet precisely because You knew that we would be the kind of creatures who would need changes of seasons and especially the coming of spring.

I think that it is very much part of Your plan. I mean, I know that everything is part of Your plan but, as I try to cope with You, I think some things in the plan are more deliberate than others. Therefore the tilt is certainly in that latter category.

Maybe You laugh at our spring worship—the day of spring music on FM yesterday. All that sound merely because of a tilt. But if You do laugh I'm sure it's an affectionate and even proud laugh: Your children have found a way to be poetic and musical about a minor orbital phenomenon—and to see You (at least implicitly) at work in that phenomenon.

I started to read last night while I was waiting for election returns from Chicago a collection of quotes from Cardinal Newman. He argues to Your existence from the voice of conscience, an argument to which I have never paid much attention which does not even now have much appeal—though I am prepared to admit that it is not without its power. I much prefer, as You well know, various forms of the nature "argument"—the sacramentality of natural phenomena and of human love.

Fortunately for us, You have revealed Yourself in many different ways for the many different kinds of people we are.

For that I thank You and for the coming of spring and for the warm weather—even if I return to Chicago on Friday to a snowstorm.

March 22

MY last day in Tucson. It's been a less than perfect interlude, but I think I've learned a lot by reflecting on it in these morning sessions. The difficulties come not from my own work which hasn't been all that great but from the demands of the phone (which I don't have to answer) and from the demands of people here for lunch and supper which are pretty hard to control. The most serious difficulty is my own inability to keep internal peace in time of stress. The best times for peace, I guess, are June and September at Grand Beach when there are no other people around. Unfortunately June is already cut up by the need to come into Chicago.

The last few days here are what the whole season should be. If the truth be told, however, there never will be that much peace in my life again. What I have will come from more rigorous screening of the outside world and more careful monitoring of my own interior state. Obviously both are important but the latter is the more important. However, I'll need lots of help to improve on that.

Next week will not be easy. In effect I'm going to be on the go at book promotion rate for four days. The difficulty, as You well know, is physical exhaustion from four flights in four days. I don't have any answers to that yet.

Anyway, thanks for the good times here. I'm sorry that I didn't do as well as I might to make the most of them. Help me and protect me in the days and weeks ahead.

Especially help me to understand how trivial are my human concerns—legitimate and necessary indeed but not terribly important in the long run.

March 23

IT'S going to be 90 again in Tucson today, and in the 20s and snow tonight in Chicago. I don't like leaving here but I'll be glad to get home.

For Chicago is home, the place where I belong. Oddly the passage in Mark's Gospel this morning recounts Jesus' return to his home in Nazareth where he had become even less popular than I am with some folk in Chicago. Indeed the animosity and envy which I encounter in my own city and from my own Archdiocese and at my own newspaper are all relatively minor compared to what Jesus endured—mostly I suppose because Jesus was so much better a person than I am.

I conclude that I am very fortunate to have so many friends and admirers and lovers in the city. For this support system—which is both extensive and intensive—I am very grateful. Help me never to let any of them down.

Thank You again for the weeks in Tucson and for the years I have spent here, years which have surely contributed to my health and happiness.

These transition times are always difficult, the old routines must be relearned, the bags must be unpacked and the boxes and their contents put in places where I have half a chance of remembering them when I want them. The mail must be opened. People must be called. And, as almost always, I must get ready for another trip. It's not easy to be serene under such circumstances. In fact I certainly won't be serene. But I don't have to blow my cool completely either. So far today so good, even if I am forgetting things every time I move.

March 24

IT'S still winter here in Chicago, but nonetheless I'm happy to be back. Like I think I said yesterday, this is where I belong. Thank You for Chicago.

Both my reading in Mark and the gospel tonight for the Mass at St. Mary of the Woods deal with men who are born blind and given sight. There is a lot less physical blindness in the world today than there used to be, thanks to medical science and to You who gave scientists the wit and the ingenuity to eliminate most blindness from the human condition (in the developed world, I hasten to add). I'm not sure whether spiritual blindness has diminished all that much. Maybe a little because of the teaching of Your Son. Nonetheless there is still a lot of it around.

Including in me.

The two gospel stories are only secondarily about the physical miracle Jesus worked, especially the story from John's Gospel on which I will preach tonight. Physical blindness in the Gospels is a symbol, a metaphor for spiritual blindness, for the inability to see what life means. Jesus came especially to heal that in all of us.

Clear enough and not disputable. How many of us priests have preached that theme time and time again and always put the spiritual blindness in the people and not in ourselves, even though we were blind to what the people thought and felt and even to the fact that they found our preaching BORING!

Do I see what life means?

Well, the best answer I can give is sometimes. When I stop to think about it, when I'm not rushing around, when I'm not tired, when I'm in a good mood, when I'm not caught in transition between Tucson and Chicago, etc.

In a sense, it's all Your fault!

You made us sensitive, agile, imaginative creatures who are so easily occupied and preoccupied with the problems, challenges, excitements, worries, agonies of this life. You expect us to respond to the phenomena around us with ingenuity and concern. Yet You also expect us not to be blind to the transiency of these phenomena, no matter how imperious their demands seem to be.

Might I say, with all due respect, that it's a tall order, an imperative that we balance the unbalanceable—this life and the Ultimate.

You know, I think You enjoy watching us try.

Maybe that's the name of the game, maybe our life is a struggle for double vision, to see and at the same time to See, to respond with all possible talent and concern to our daily problems and still to see That which lurks beneath them and beyond them.

You, in other words.

So in the midst of my rushing around today, help me to think of You more often than usual.

March 25

I AM told by today's gospel reading that I must lose my life in order to find it, by Professor Nozick that I must seek to become most real, by the poet I'm reading to imitate Whitman's contentment with a simple life and finally by the psalmist that I am a little less than the angels.

Now, I ask, can I do and be all those things at the same time? The advise from all four sources is good advice, but how do I balance all of them? How do I engage in what seems real to me, namely writing and research and story telling and live a simple and uncomplicated life?

How do I give up self and still remember that I am only a little less than an angel?

Or am I most real when I am most like an angel and that is doing that which seems to me to be best and avoiding worry and strain which seems to interfere with or be generated by doing that which is real?

Fine, that seems to be good advice, but hardly a recipe for a simple life. Can one be real and still be detached? Or is it the other way around? When I am most detached, am I most real?

Detachment means not to care about the outcome, does it not? But how can I not care about the outcome of the many projects in which I am currently engaged? If all You mean is that I should not let undue concern about outcomes interfere with my peace of mind, I have no problem, except where does "undue" differ from "due"?

I am leaving tomorrow on a tour to promote the new book—in itself hardly an exercise of a simple life but an obligation which seems to go with being a writer. Does detachment from the result of this tour and the success of the book mean indifference to these events? I think not.

But what then is the boundary line between indifference and detachment, between involvement and the simple life?

Can I even define that difference?

Does all this advice merely mean that I should try not to lose my cool? It certainly does not mean that I shouldn't have the projects I do, though perhaps it does mean that I ought not to overextend myself. But how do I know when I'm overextended?

At a minimum, the conclusion must be that I should

not let defeat or failure or rejection deprive me of my peace or prevent me from trying something else. The peace point is well taken, but rejection doesn't really deprive me of peace for very long, or I would have quit long ago.

Perhaps the only conclusion is that all this advice, like all proverbs, is not magical and needs to be applied prudently and cautiously in the particular set of circumstances in which I find myself. An Arizona basketball game, in which I can become pretty involved while it is going on, is not the same as being on the Today Show. To be more involved in the outcome of the latter than the outcome of the former is not at all unreasonable.

And, here is the point that I think is crucial and to which I will return tomorrow: the less worried I am about that (up to the point where no adrenalin flows) the more successful the interview will be.

Teach me, in Eliot's words, to care and not to care.

March 26

AS part of my conflict with the transition strain I went to two films yesterday—*Joe and the Vocano* and *Pretty Woman*; they were both love stories if somewhat off-beat love stories. Also, each in its own way, was a morality play about not wasting Your life, the protagonist for the former in timidity and the latter in ambition. Once again the popular culture reenforces religious values which are at odds with the work values honored by society.

They fit nicely with my present concern about what is "real" and about being prepared to lose my life so as to gain it—the latter being the precise and explicit theme of *Joe.*

Nozick, in the conclusion of his chapter on the real, notes that we are most real not only in our "peak" experiences but also in our "depth" experiences, when we are at our maximum and also at our most intensely reflective. Both situations represent a break-away from the ordinary routines of life. I certainly have enough maximum experiences as I write and work with problems and tell stories. My depth experiences are less frequent but they are present at least on occasion.

These latter are the kinds of experiences like Jesus had in the Transfiguration as reported in today's gospel reading, experiences that bring one close to You and transform the personality and the character and help one to *know* and *see.* I've never quite had a mystical experience, but I have had experiences of depth in which I begin to *see.*

All of these sources seem to point to a warning against the ordinary, against letting the routine of life interfere with the peak and the depth moments. Giving up one's life means, among other things, having the courage to break away from the ordinary, routine fears and concerns to be open to height and depth.

That's a stern judgment on me. While my routine is exciting, it is still routine. Help me in the days and weeks ahead, especially on this nutty promotion tour, to let the non-ordinary, the extraordinary, into my life.

Andrew Greeley

March 27

I WAS in fine shape at the doctor's yesterday—four pounds lighter and perfect blood pressure. Moreover I feel fine, even into this trip.

However, he wants a colon exam—for my peace of mind since he insists he is satisfied with blood culture tests. There's no sign of anything but, since my mother died of it (among other things) he says I'll be more relaxed if I don't have the worry. I suppose he's right, though to tell the truth I wasn't all that worried. We'll do the test in June, which gives me two and a half months to think about it. Somehow my schedule always precludes having tests right away and getting them over with. There always seems to be a trip to Europe that intervenes. I wonder if my schedule will ever permit me time to die!

How should I react to the coming of this examination? First of all, Marty Phee has never been wrong before and he is not concerned. Secondly, if there is something inside of me, it's most fortunate to get it early. Thirdly, if the seeds of my death lurk in my body then I am no different from anyone else, since we are all born to die. Finding out about the specific agent of my own mortality will only make the time and the cause of my death more precise. Hence there ought not to be anything to worry about—we'll either find nothing to worry about or we will have greater certainty about dying which might just as well be done and gotten over with.

Am I really that confident? That serene?

Well, perhaps not. But I don't propose to be preoccupied about the examination. When it comes it will come and the outcome is already written. I will learn about it in due time and not try to anticipate its findings.

The superstitious Irish in me says that if You don't worry that's a sure sign there'll be something to worry about—an instinct that God punishes those who do not worry. You're not that sort of Person at all, and I reject the instinct.

The fact of this examination does, however, put a new perspective on my current trip and on my reflections about the meaning of reality. Death is the ultimate reality that we know. You transcend death and I will know You more intimately after death. By "ultimate" I mean final. I will have to go through it some time sooner or later. I must leave to Your love and Your promise of help the how and the when.

We're being delayed over paper-work because of new light blubs in the plane. That's not very important either, is it?

March 28

IT'S Wednesday so it must be Boston. I'm in a green room again, with Jason Robards and Elaine Stritch across the way. What a character she is! But both of them are Catholics and very respectful to a priest. I told her that her cousin ordained me and she seemed delighted. She is at least as manic in person as she is in her roles and he is even more laid back.

Anyway, I'll try to reflect despite her noise. I'm not worn out yet, probably because the Arizona stint was more relaxing than I had thought it was. It's kind of interesting to compare this tour with the early ones. I'm no longer particuarly nervous and certainly not intimidated by the interviewers or the callers. I've learned to be cool on the cool medium. The new religion writer at the *Washington Post* asked me whether I was promoting religion or myself on the programs—a direct enough question. I replied that I was promoting the book because my publishers expected that I do so and that I also thought it was good to have a priest on radio and TV in the secular world.

I confess I enjoy the give and take of the interviews, they're like the old oral exams in the seminary. It's the traveling and the waiting and the packing and unpacking that wear me out and eventually disorient me.

There is a kind of discouragement in all of this, not merely because the questions are the same and because I seem older and more battered—and more mortal—than I had been ten years ago. Despite my answer to the reporter in Washington, I find being a celebrity—something I didn't choose to be—a cheapening experience. There are a lot of better things to be done with time it seems to me. It goes with the territory I guess. Sometimes it all seems futile and degrading. What difference does it make? But what difference does anything make? All You can do is try.

Yet the interest of the interviewers (In Boston they're all Catholic, naturally) and the call-ins suggests that there is still enormous vitality in the Church despite the hierarchy.

Anyway it's an interesting life and I'm not complaining about Your plans for me. I have no doubt that You want me to be here and represent You as best I can and as imperfectly as I do. I'm grateful that so far I don't take myself seriously in this role. I'd be surprised if I ever do.

Help me to remember in the course of the day who I am and whom I represent, as I say, however imperfectly.

March 29

A QUARTER to seven in the morning on the last day of this mini-tour for *The Catholic Myth*. Since I can't swim this morning, I'm up early before the Today Show to write these reflections and take a long walk. All part of my new program of exercise and prayer early in the morning. So far it has helped though it does not offset the ill effects of being in an airplane every day.

Reaction to the book from interviewers has been very positive indeed, though I have no illusions that it will have much of an impact on either those media types who believe the myth or those church leaders who believe it. However, one does what one can.

At least Catholicism is still news as someone remarked yesterday—still news because it is still alive and vital and turbulent. I had supper with Jim Mahoney last night and he gave me the dedication book of the new church in his parish—seventeen saints not including the ones in the stained glass and a May crowning next month. Mary the Mother of Jesus is still popular with people, though it will take a long time before the clergy and the theologians rediscover her and the saints, to say nothing of the Catholic imagination which sees the world filled with sacraments of You.

I have tried to remember through this trip who and what I am and not to let weariness and discouragement take away my peace and patience, especially on mike or camera. It's easier under such circumstances than when stalled in a check-in line, but so far I'm doing OK. What happens on a longer tour will be another matter.

Every once in a while I pause to marvel that I had never expected in my life to do any of these things, yet here I am doing maybe my twentieth Today Show and having lunch with the editors of the *New York Times Magazine*. It is an opportunity to represent the Church in this world of the upper media, an opportunity for which the old theory of the presence of the Church in the world would cheer, even if the present theorists resent the fact that I can do it.

There are times when I felt thoroughly isolated and cut off and other times when I feel close to the center of the Church.

I'm rambling again because I am tired and with the weariness depressed. I do love You. I know that You do love me. Take care of me for the rest of the day and bring me home safely tonight.

March 30

I AM exhausted from the the trip. Yesterday was pretty bad, particularly the plane flight back from New York. I had planned to head for Grand Beach, but there's rain and fog and it will continue through the whole weekend. So I'll stay here and read and swim and maybe go to a movie. I travel badly and not all the exercise or the reflections in the world are going to change that. I feel drained, degraded, wasted. It's an emotional reaction I know and I'll be better in a day or two. I simply have to arrange my traveling so there's time to relax at either end. This time all I have to do is catch up on the mail and complete the transition here.

March 31

IT'S been a long time since I took off a day like today and did nothing but read and watch TV. I didn't leave the apartment, not even to swim. In the past when I went to Grand Beach more frequently in the winter I did such days more often. They're wonderful, particularly after four airplane flights in four days. A good way to end March and to end wintertime.

I thank You for this day of healthy collapse. Help me to do it more often.

I'll be back tomorrow to recollect on Your son's healing those who were mentally ill and what that means in the life of a priest today.

April 1

THE reading in the gospel today shows Your Son casting out demons, which, I presume, means curing people who were mentally ill—a much greater accomplishment than curing physical illness. It raises the question of how we respond to neurosis in ourselves and in others. It also raises the question of why You permit neurosis to constrain so much talent and creativity and so much potential for happiness in this world.

When I was ordained, the notion of psychological impairment of freedom was held by only a minority of priests, even a minority of my generation. Rarely would we suggest that someone be sent to a psychiatrist and more rarely would the advice be followed. I still remember the woman who almost walked out of the office when I suggested her boy needed some "counseling."

Did he ever! And she was the cause!

Scarcely five years later we had a psychiatric seminary and Catholics were going off to see therapists and analysts (even) at the same rate Jews were. I was sending young men and women to analysts from the Institute and at a steady rate—without much success as it turns out. From believing that one could solve anything by will power we became a culture where human responsibility was so diminished that it virtually never existed. We had been able to excuse nothing, now we excused everything.

The psychiatric church continues. But where is the middle ground, since we cannot cast out the demon of mental illness as quickly as Jesus did?

I don't know the answer to that. I do know, however, that while priests must always be sympathetic to the pain that (we) neurotics feel and be prepared to admit that in God's eyes moral responsibility is often diminished, we must nonetheless insist on responsible behavior, we must assume that most people are capable of being responsible adults and hold them to adult behavior in their relationships with us. We must not permit neurotic excuses lest we merely feed the neuroticism itself.

Nor must we use them to excuse ourselves.

That's a tough principle, especially when some therapists tell clients (or appear to tell clients) and relatives that the neurotic excuse is valid for "the time being." Standing for reality without being punitive about it is not an easy task, nor one that is easily understood.

I acknowledge all my failures in this area, sometimes too lenient, sometimes too tough, and also admit I still don't have any clue as to how to respond to many situations. How do You say, "I love You and I care about You, but don't try to manipulate me with Your neurosis?"

I don't know. I guess I must continue to proceed by trial and error.

I think especially of all those young people I tried to save from family-induced neuroses—foolishly, in retrospect, because what can a priest do against a family, especially an internalized family. They are no longer young and most of them are terribly unhappy now. I didn't make them any more troubled (save perhaps marginally) but I didn't help them much either.

Moreover, if I had it to do over, I don't see what I might do differently that would help them, other than to have removed myself from their lives earlier so that I would not be an ink blot for their problems.

This is a melancholy reflection for another gray and foggy day. Help those poor people whom I still love and whom, I know, You love even more than I do.

Andrew Greeley

April 2

THE fog and the rain continue in Chicago. Four straight days. Most depressing. I sound like President Bush, don't I?

The subject today is values—what is the dominant goal and motivation of my life, not in some theoretical statement but in practice.

Since I was a little boy the goal has been to be a good priest, to teach and preach Catholicism. My stories and my sociology are nothing more than roles in which that goal can be served. I have not always pursued those values with the purity and clarity with which I might have pursued them. I have permitted myself to be distracted by means to those values, often to the extent of losing sight of the values themselves. But they are still the dominant values of my life. Everything I do is oriented, however imperfectly at times and however remotely at other times, to those goals.

April 3

PREACHING the good news of Your love for us is the central value of my life, the concern around which all others should revolve and to some extent do revolve. My novels are stories about Your love. It is necessary that I assert that in the face of gratuitous and dishonest attacks of those who cannot or will not see that obvious fact. But it is not necessary or appropriate that such defense become as important as it has become for me - understandable indeed but not appropriate or necessary.

I do believe in Your love and preaching it is the central value of my life, but I do not believe in it strongly enough to sustain me during the inevitable hard times. Therefore I must conclude with the prayer that You increase my love in response to Your love so that there will be more peace and joy in my life, even if I am beleaguered.

April 4

I'M still kind of worn out from the tour which was now almost a week ago. I had to come back to the apartment twice today after reaching the ground, once for the books I was going to give Dick Phelan for a birthday present and the other time for my wallet—I had almost entered the cab.

The fog and the rain are back, maybe that's part of the problem.

Anyway, back to values. I learned yesterday that my memoir had virtually earned out its advance which made it a very successful book indeed. That fact made me moderately happy, not ecstatically so, but it was a nice feeling that the company had not invested its money in vain.

With the new novel appearing, I hope that it does well, that the reviews are straight, that the tour goes well, and that readers like the story. These are all values to me, I think I might even say important values. They come with being an author. Of course I want my books to be read. To claim that I do not would be dishonest and also a pretense at piety which would be phony. Everyone who writes wants to be read and enjoyed.

However, these values are intermediate, not ultimate. The trick is to keep them solidly in the intermediate range and to prevent them from becoming ultimate values or values that are so important that they weaken other and richer and more important values.

As I hardly need tell You, the human organism does not do that either easily or pefectly. It takes constant energy and effort to keep one's values in a properly ordered hierarchy and the outcome of the energy and effort is always substantially short of ideal.

I think I can see that these intermediate values have never gotten wildly out of hand. You blessed me with too much common sense for me to let that happen. Or maybe too many other things to ever be distracted completely by disappointments in intermediate values. I'd love to have a film made from one of my stories. I'd love to write the script for the film. But there's no danger of that desire ever becoming an obsession.

However, I know as well as You do how easily I become discouraged about my work, how quickly I slip over into a kind of depression (particularly on days like this). You also know about my Depression era pessimism. Help me in the weeks ahead to be clear enough about my ultimate values so that they dominate the rest of my life—especially when I'm weary and groggy like I am today.

April 6

THERE is something inherently restful about Grand Beach. I forget what it is like until I'm here and have a restful night's sleep. It helps that the sun is out too. Such a creature of light and environment am I.

Anyway it's a wonderful breather from the craziness of the last two weeks and of the weeks yet to come. I wonder if I can get back here before June 1—what a terrible admission.

Much of the trouble the last couple of days came from rushing out for breakfast without getting my life in order first, but I was in desperate need of sleep.

Days like that happen, but is it my fault that weeks happen? Should I be going to Europe at the end of this month with the tour for my new novel? The subject of the meeting in Graz is religion, I really should be there. I could fly there and back and miss Prague and Budapest and Dublin, but I don't want to do that.

There's the value issue right out in the open, isn't it? I value the book tour (because everyone says I should). I value the trip because it will be interesting and sociologically necessary. I value Grand Beach.

Nozick, who raised this question for me in his book, cops out at the end by saying that we must harmonize and balance all our values. Thanks a lot.

In other words, there is not much wisdom in addition to the conventional wisdom. All of this work is part of being a priest the way I have been chosen to be a priest. Like it or not, I must endure the next eight weeks—and with as much calm and cheer as I can, trying to keep in mind what the mission and value is that integrates all of them.

I must also be content with my own imperfections in carrying out and balancing these multiple responsibilities—knowing that You love me no matter how I mess up.

Also I'll try to figure out a way to get up here at Easter. Thank You for these two days.

April 7

TOMORROW is Palm Sunday. Lent has slipped by all too quickly. One of the many disadvantages of not being part of one regular parish is that I find it hard to be part of the rhythm of the liturgical year. I suppose that's true of the laity too for the most part. Moreover Holy Week means less to me since I have stopped living in a rectory. I'm going to do my best to make the evening services at SMW this week but it's going to be a busy week as I prepare for the trip to Europe and work on the various projects which must be cleared away before I leave—while all the time losing large parts of the day to the various lunches and suppers which I must attend. Again I beg You to help me through the next two months. And help me to figure out how I got into this mess.

I don't have to figure that out. I've spent all week working on it in these reflections. I overcommitted myself and, given the opportunities, I'd probably do it all again.

Last night I watched *Big* on cable, a marvelous film about childhood and the importance of preserving the child in all of us when we become adults. Twice in a week films have made this point to me—*Ninja Turtles* last week.

Did not Your son say the same thing—we must become like little children if we are to enter the kingdom of heaven. I presume he meant the same thing the two film-makers meant: the child lives in a world of wonder and surprise and excitement, of fun and opportunity, of cele bration and fun.

We are all too serious. Yesterday I reread my article in *U.S. Catholic* that Catholics have more fun. They do indeed and often. Yet if we really believed in Your love we'd have more fun, there'd be more wonder and surprise in our lives.

As I look out the window here at Grand Beach and see the green grass, the barren trees, the purple branches of the lilacs—which I think were caught in the false spring a month ago—I remember Chesterton's famous line about the coming of spring every year suggests a plot and a Plotter. Obviously the latter is You. And just as obviously You cause spring through the wobble of the earth on its axis. However, even if it is a cliche, the coming of spring is full of wonder. Yet I pay so little attention to its wonder, especially because I'm likely to be in an airplane somewhere when it's happening.

These next eight weeks are going to be very busy. I'm likely to be exhausted and depressed much of the time. In the midst of it all please keep alive my capacity for and sense of wonder.

Andrew Greeley

April 8, Palm Sunday

THE classic meditation on this day is still a good one—the crowds cheered on Palm Sunday for Your son. A few days later they called for his death. It may well be that there were different people in the two crowds. Perhaps the crowd who demanded death were plants like the crowds in Eastern Europe before the collapse of Communism. Yet one would still have to ask, where were those who cheered on Palm Sunday?

The perhaps melancholy conclusion one must come to is that there are not very many people on whom You can count when the lights go out.

I have found that out the hard way repeatedly in the course of my life. Oddly, even though I knew better, I was still surprised when it happened. Not everyone deserts You; there are always the loyalists. But a lot do, even some on whom You thought You could count—and some of that latter are in the crowd shouting "Crucify!" Some You thought were friends are even organizing the crowd.

Like I say, I knew in principle that the human condition was that way and that the Palm Sunday/Good Friday pardigm applies to everyone and not just to Jesus. Still I guess You have to experience it Yourself to really believe it. Then You can refuse to trust anyone ever again or feel sorry for Yourself or turn bitter and angry.

I am prepared to admit that I did not completely resist any of those three temptations. Indeed I am still subject to them. I haven't succumbed to them completely but they are still part of my life and, I suppose, always will be.

As Your son knew, one feels terribly deserted and alone after such events—betrayed, cut off, isolated, foresaken to use the words of the scripture. All that is left is You. That is enough, that is everything, but I perceive that only dimly, as much as I believe it to be true.

Strengthen my faith in Your protecting love, please, please. Otherwise, bitterness and anger will continue to haunt me and Easter will recede further into the distance. Only when anger is conquered (though not eliminated as a temptation) only then does one rise from the dead.

And the conquest of anger depends finally on how much I can throw myself on the power and passion of Your love.

April 9

AS Holy Week begins on this gray Monday morning— the sun has forgotten about Chicago—I want to try to bring myself closer to the spirit of the time even though at my distance from parish life, it does not mean what it used to mean.

In the research I'm doing now on Chicago Catholics I have found that the biggest reason they give for being Catholic is "the sacraments," described by more than four-fifths of the respondents as "very important" in their Catholicism. David Tracy is right about us being a sacramental people and so is my sociological version of the theory. Sacramentality is at the essence of Catholicism. It's one more aspect of the faith of the people to which the leadership pays little attention.

I wonder how much Holy Week figures in that sacramentality of the people. Not very much perhaps because so few of them (relatively) make it to Church on Thursday and Friday. However, Palm Sunday and Easter do matter and both are feasts of celebration. Holy Week ought to be a time of joy and penance, and more joy than penance. I'm going to fast this week as best I can given my schedule for the penance part and I'm going to try to be more joyous for the joy part despite the bind of obligations and schedules in which I am caught.

I don't feel very joyous this morning at 7:00 with a trip to the dentist ahead, the worst way that I know of to begin a day, except maybe a business breakfast. But there is much to rejoice about—Jesus is risen and You love all of us.

April 10

MY LOVE,

Yesterday I came upon the ultimate sacrament book—*14,000 Things to be Happy About* by Barbara Ann Kipper. For twenty years she has kept a list of wonderful things to be found in the world. Thus on the first page (of 612) she lists among other things, "reed fringed lagoons," "seeing the moon rise," "shadows cast by shutters against shiny white walls," and "the feel of a rug under bare feet."

Right!

I'm going to buy a dozen or so and pass them around to family and friends. As Catholics we have to believe that everyone of her 14,000 things are a hint of Your goodness, Your beauty, Your loving presence in the world.

YEAR OF GRACE

What a marvelously sensitive and perceptive person the author must be to have remembered and written down all those happy-making things, all those sacraments. And how dull I have become to barely notice such wonders. I'm sorry, I truly am.

The psalmist leaves off today from ranting at his enemies long enough to speak movingly of his thirst for You. We all thirst for You. You have made us for Yourself alone and we are thristy until we drink the waters of the spring of Your love. All those wonders with which we are surrounded are tidbits, appetitizers, come-ons, vague traces of Your creative presence.

By now I presume the spaceship Discovery is in orbit with the Hubble telescope which will enable the astronomers to see perhaps as far away as ten billion light years—back perhaps even to the Big Bang. I have this wonderfully irrelevant and I hope not irreverent fantasy that they'll finally catch a glimpse of You with a big grin on Your face as You started all the fun.

Seriously I can't escape the notion that You enjoyed and enjoy creation enormously and that You enjoy (and respect) our faltering efforts to comprehend it. Like the reeds and the rug under bare feet, the Big Bang is a whiff of Your presence and Your love, so powerful, so passionate that we cannot begin to grasp what it is like. I personally prefer the rug and the reeds and the rising of the moon to the Big Bang, despite my poems about the Big Bang, because they show a nice attention to detail. It's not an industrial-strength cosmos You've produced but rather one that is tidy and pretty even in its most minute aspects. You do all things well.

Help me to appreciate the promiscuity of Your love,

lavished on creation and on us with reckless affection. Help me to to be happy about all these wonderful gifts and to share that happiness with others.

April 11

MY LOVE,

It has been a disconcerting experience to read through the year of these reflections. On the one hand I sound more pious than I feel. On the other I seem to complain an awful lot about the pressures of time and weariness and discouragement and anger. I don't find the person in the journal all that attractive.

Well, at least I didn't pull any punches or try to make myself look good. I wrote what was on my mind. I did take seriously my belief that You love me regardless of how I feel or what I say.

Love is never easy, it does not run away from the faults of the beloved. So You won't run away from my faults, no matter how unappealing they may make me.

I'll have to absorb what this journal means and reflect on it for several days. Obviously some things in my life must be changed. It's been helpful to articulate my feelings and reactions on paper. I think I'm in better emotional condition now than I was a year ago when I began to write. But still there is a grimness about my life which is totally inappropriate for someone caught up in a love affair with You. As I said so often in the course of writing I do believe that You are a passionate, vulnerable, caring lover who for some astonishing reason needs me. To love the character that has written this journal is surely to be open to the charge of craziness, a charge which You have never denied in Your love affairs with us.

This Holy Week will be a good time to reflect deeply on the meaning of life and my love affair with You—even if I am overwhelmed with work, with lunch and dinner responsibilities, and with preparations for the trip to Europe.

I know You don't mind my complaining. I know that one of the roles of prayer is honest communication with a lover. But there ought to be more celebration in our "pillow talk." I suppose that's the big lack in this journal—not enough joy and celebration.

The theme which runs through it constantly is that there is not enough time. What a stupid excuse for not having enough joy and celebration in my life.

I'm very sorry. I do love You. Help me to love You more.

Some friends from the old group were very much on my mind. Please take care of them and help the.

April 12, Holy Thursday

I finished rereading this journal last night and am less discouraged by it and by me than I was yesterday. I lead a hectic, harassed, volatile life. It's inevitable given who and what I am. There's nothing wrong with that so long as I try to keep in mind the fact that You love me and that it is in response to Your love that I work. Keeping this journal is an important part of my life and I must continue to do it every morning insofar as I can.

Today is the feast of the priesthood, not that I take

seriously the old notion that Jesus "ordained" his followers at the Last Supper the way Cardinal Stritch ordained me back in 1954. But the Eucharist began at least in a certain sense at the seder on Holy Thursday and with the Eucharist there came the role of the religious leader who presides over the Eucharist.

One of the major findings of the research on the Archdiocese in which I am currently engaged is that the parish priest is enormously important to Catholics. So what else is new? Except somehow priests don't seem to comprehend that fact. Morale is so poor and self-pity so strong that the needs of the laity don't seem to get through or to enter into the calculus. Few if any of the sessions of senates or priest councils either locally or nationally pay any attention to the needs of the laity, so busy are they with the right of priests.

The priesthood is in disarray, short of leadership, short of zeal, short of vision—and paralyzed by mediocrity. That statement applies today but I guess it could apply equally as well to the crowd around the table at the Last Supper, couldn't it?

I like being a priest; I don't doubt my vocation to the priesthood; I have no regrets; I believe in the priesthood now more than I ever did. I am grateful to You for my vocation. With Your help I will never turn away from it. I am one of the fortunate ones and I want never to forget that: my vision of the priesthood has never changed. Grant that it never will change.

So I renew in this reflection what I will renew publically tonight at SMW: I commit myself again to the priesthood. Help me to be a good priest.

And take care of my fellow priests who are so confused

and so discouraged and so resentful. Above all grant them hope and joy and the leadership which they have not had now for decades.

I have resolved as I read the "happy" book to note two causes of happiness each day. Yesterday I rejoiced in the taste of chocolate and of the fruit plate at Escargot.

Interesting that I would start with food, isn't it?

Today my first "happy" is Holy Thursday and the second is the priesthood.

April 13, Good Friday

MY LOVE,

As You know, I decided that just as Your Son did what had to be done on Good Friday, so I must do what had to be done, that is work on the Chicago project which has to be in on Monday if they are going to have time to get it ready for publication before I leave for Europe. That was that.

I did manage to do the first draft of all seven articles. Tomorrow I will revise and do some charts and devote time, with Your help, to the celebration of the Passover Triduum.

This was the worst day for love in all of history and also the best day—the worst because Love died and Love was not able to protect it from death. And the best day because it was demonstrated on Calvary how far Love would go to prove itself, how vulnerable You would make Yourself to tell us how much You needed our love.

Even to write those two sentences is to plunge so deeply into the mystery of what life and creation mean as to take my breath away. How can You be so vulnerable? How can You permit it? How could You tolerate Love, admittedly Your Love, going so far?

And yet You suffer not only with Jesus but with every ugly evil human suffering that mars Your splendid creation. You would have to be infinite to be able to suffer so much.

I was glancing at the Oxford prayer book while the machine was producing something else. All about immensity in these pages—and immense You certainly are. I don't find that so appealing as Your intimacy, as You well know. But immensity is still part of You. Yet so much suffering for immensity! So much suffering that only immensity can absorb it all!

I'm too tired tonight to try to figure this out, no, I can't figure it out, to reflect on it. I'll be back tomorrow.

Happy things for the day—finishing a project and its problems, and relaxing in a swimming pool in the midst of a day of intense work.

April 14, Holy Saturday

IF yesterday was the day of the death of love and the triumph of love, today is the day of the beginning of the resurgence of love. The other night I watched the Russian film *Little Vera*. As a portrait of life in the Soviet Union today it was dismaying—Gorbachev has a long road ahead of him to reform and civilize that country and to make it less depressing.

But the film was about love among the members of the family and between Vera and her boyfriend. The characters were men and women with little impulse control and a propensity for too much of the drink which would make the Irish seem sober by comparison. They did terrible things emotionally and physically to one another. Yet at the end there was love among them all. Love, and not a pretty version of it either, had somehow triumphed.

Our deepest human instincts say that this is true despite all the evil in the world, despite tragedy, suffering and death, despite heartache, disappointment, frustration. I think of some of my friends from the past whose married love has torn itself apart in neurotic conflict, conflict generated by their own free-will decisions. I think of all the family conflicts in which love has been battered by sibling rivalry and envy.

Love still perdures. It does not win in every case—and its victory in the Russian film was at best temporary and imperfect. Yet it at least has the power to win, to defeat conflict and anger and hurt and eventually even death.

That power is latent in the human condition. At this time of the year we celebrate it's validation in the Resurrection of Jesus, a triumph not only of life over death but of love over hate. You have validated in the Jesus event not only the resiliency of love but its ultimate power.

I believe that on this gray, rainy Holy Saturday morning. I know that my Redeemer lives and that I too live and shall live, no matter what happens. Strengthen my faith and my love for You. And deepen my insight into the truth that You suffer with all of us and not only with Jesus, that Your sufferings are the raw material out of which Resurrection is made.

The fire and water brought together tonight mean life, the rebirth and renewal of life, life bought at a price, life perilously clung to, yet life victorious.

April 15, Easter Sunday

TODAY is the end of my first year of keeping this journal of religious reflections. It has been an extremely helpful idea, one for which I thank You very much. Dan Herr wants to get out an edited version. It's fine with me. I'm sure You don't mind others listening to our conversations.

Resurrection isn't supposed to be easy. So says Noel Farrell in my favorite novel, *Lord of the Dance.* As in most matters Noel is right. How do You celebrate holidays when You are exhausted from the celebration—a variant of the earlier problem of why Christmas has to come during the Holidays. I've spent much of the day in the car riding back and forth to St. Mary of the Woods and the Durkin house and was sleepy because the party in the apartment next door kept me awake most of the night. Under such circumstances it is all well and good to say in Your head that this is the feast of the Resurrection of the Lord, but survival till You can get a chance to sleep becomes the main preoccupation.

The weaknesses of human nature, not its sinfulnes but its limitations, its propensity to weariness and exhaustion, interfere with its spiritual aspirations. As they said when the idiocies of the sixties "revolutions" began to wind down, even revolutionaries need to sleep.

YEAR OF GRACE

So, too, do those who want to rejoice in the resurrection.

There was nonetheless lots of celebration in the services at SMW and at the party at the Durkins'. So the trick is to ride the wave of celebration in such circumstances and revel in it even if you're too beat to reflect much on what is happening. That's all I could do today and I know that's enough for You who love me despite all my limitations.

The Masses were well nigh perfect, particularly the vigil which was only a few minutes too long and was carried out with grace and charm and emphasis on joy rather than on liturgical kinkiness, like the one in Tucson last year. I found myself smiling spontaneously despite my yawns through most of it.

I believe that Your son rose from the dead and that we celebrated not only his triumph over death but our own. Some day I will conquer death just like he did and, as Leo said in the sermon, walk through the door to a new and categorically different kind of life. Help me to believe that more strongly and to permit that belief to permeate my life.

And that is as good a way as any to end this year of grace.